Presented to:

_____

From:

_____

Date:

_____

101 Amazing Things About Heaven

❧

*Discover the Surprising
Truth About Heaven and
How You Can Get There*

HONOR ⌷ BOOKS
FROM DAVID C. COOK

101 AMAZING THINGS ABOUT HEAVEN
Published by Honor Books®, an imprint of
David C. Cook
4050 Lee Vance View
Colorado Springs, CO 80918 U.S.A.

David C. Cook Distribution Canada
55 Woodslee Avenue, Paris, Ontario, Canada N3L 3E5

David C. Cook U.K., Kingsway Communications
Eastbourne, East Sussex BN23 6NT, England

David C. Cook and the graphic circle C logo
are registered trademarks of Cook Communications Ministries.

ISBN 978-1-56292-230-6

© 2004 Bordon Books
Manuscript written by Robin Schmidt
Developed by Bordon Books
6532 E. 71st Street, Suite 105
Tulsa, OK 74133

Cover Photo: ©digitialvision

Printed in Canada
First Edition 2007

6 7 8 9 10 11 12

090907

Introduction

No one but Jesus is qualified to say what heaven is really like. However, God has revealed many amazing facts about heaven in the Scriptures, and He's blessed us with the incredible gift of imagination. We believe He invites us to let our imagination soar as we consider with fascination and wonder these astounding biblical truths. Our hope and prayer is that the thoughts expressed in this book will spark your own imaginings, cause your heart to swell with a desire for eternity, and inspire you to live by the sure hope of God's promises.

1.

Heaven is closer than you think!

You may think heaven is far away, but Jesus said it's not. Here on earth, God's kingdom exists in the hearts of all believers. We can move closer to heaven and experience part of it even now, before Christ takes us there to live forever.

The closer you follow Jesus, the shorter the distance to heaven.

🌿

"THE KINGDOM OF HEAVEN IS NEAR."
—MATTHEW 4:17 NLT

2.
You ain't seen nothing yet!

We speak of the wonder of God's creation, yet we experience only part of it—the earth, sun, moon, and stars, the universe that surrounds us. God himself, the Maker of heaven and earth, called this part of His creation good, but it has become broken, shattered by sin, and corrupted by evil. Although it retains some of its former glory—and that alone can be stunningly beautiful—the creation we live in provides us only a suggestion of the splendor of paradise.

Our contemplation of heaven is constrained by our understanding, which is limited by our perspective. How can a caterpillar crawling along a tree branch and eating leaves have any foretaste of its life as a butterfly, when it will soar on the wind and drink the flower's sweet nectar?

We envision heaven with crystal blue skies, majestic mountains, pristine rivers, pounding ocean surf, and countless brilliant stars, yet in truth these images are but aged, yellowed photographs, their colors faded, their images blurred. They represent reality, but only barely. One day we'll set those pictures aside, gaze up, and behold a perfect heaven, a place untouched by sin, reality as God intended it, a place that only He could have created.

When you consider eternity, ask God to help you look beyond the images in your mind, even those you most dearly treasure, and remind you that heaven—like He himself—is beyond our comprehension.

❧

"NO EYE HAS SEEN, NO EAR HAS HEARD,
NO MIND HAS CONCEIVED WHAT GOD
HAS PREPARED FOR THOSE WHO LOVE HIM."
—1 CORINTHIANS 2:9

3.
The Holy City sparkles like a gem.

An urban skyline at night can be dazzling. In the darkness, multicolored lights converge to create a spectacular display, and from a high overlook the whole downtown area seems to gleam spotlessly.

However, as you drive through the streets in the daytime the city, however impressive, seems to lose its glow, and everywhere there are signs of imperfection, dirt, and decay. Older buildings look worn; occasionally one with broken windows appears abandoned and empty. Bridges and overpasses are beginning to rust. The roads have potholes here and there. Even the most thriving modern cities exhibit subtle symptoms of deterioration.

There are no such blights in the city of heaven! It never loses its luster. It has no need for the cover of night; it has no flaws to hide. The Bible says this city glistens like a jewel. But unlike earth's precious stones, which are often displayed on black velvet, this gem doesn't require a dark backdrop to accentuate its beauty. The city always shines brilliantly, even amid the resplendent, never-ending light of eternity, reflecting the glory of its Creator.

As you drive along the streets where you live, let the cracks in the pavement remind you that in heaven exists a city that, like God, sparkles with everlasting perfection.

❧

THE CITY SHIMMERED LIKE A PRECIOUS GEM, LIGHT-
FILLED, PULSING LIGHT.
—REVELATION 21:11 MSG

4.
Even the yardsticks there are made of gold.

Revelation 21:15–21 provides us with an astounding description of the city of heaven. It's made of pure gold, and the foundations of its walls are adorned with precious jewels. The city has twelve gates, each carved from a single pearl. Its main street is paved with twenty-four-carat gold, shiny as glass. In this fine city, even simple tools such as measuring sticks are made of precious metal!

God has seemingly spared no expense in creating our new home. Now, you might be thinking that it didn't cost God anything at all to make heaven for us. Perhaps you're right. After all, He is God; it's not as if He has to purchase building materials! But it did cost God everything to make heaven available to us. That cost Him the life of His only Son. First Peter 1:18–19 NRSV says God paid the price for us "not with perishable things like silver or gold, but with the precious blood of Christ." There is nothing more valuable to God, in heaven or on earth, than His Son, Jesus—and He gave Him up for our sake.

How many of us would be willing to pay such a price? Yet because God was willing to pay it, we all have the opportunity to live forever in a place where even common things are priceless.

We take a step closer to heaven when we appreciate the value of God's gift, understand what it cost Him to purchase it for us, and realize that all we have to do is gratefully accept it.

❧

THE ANGEL SPEAKING WITH ME HAD A GOLD MEASURING STICK TO MEASURE THE CITY, ITS GATES, AND ITS WALL.
—REVELATION 21:15 MSG

5.
The city of heaven is bigger than Texas.

The world has known many great cities in the past, such as ancient Rome, and modern-day metropolises that are impressive indeed. But never has there been a place like God's eternal city!

The New Jerusalem, as this amazing city is called in the Bible, is huge. Revelation 21:16 says it's 1,500 miles wide and 1,500 miles long. That's an area of over two million square miles—making the city of heaven much bigger than the Lone Star State. In fact, it's almost four times as large as the state of Alaska, over half the size of the entire United States! A city that big would be anything but crowded and uncomfortable. Surely it would be filled with flowering trees, grassy parks, expansive gardens, and broad, wonderfully landscaped boulevards.

However, if even these amazing dimensions seem too confining for a place like heaven, keep in mind that they apply only to the city; who knows the extent of the countryside?

There's one thing more: Incredibly—and this really stretches the imagination—the city is also 1,500 miles high. Truly heaven is beyond our comprehension!

We all yearn for more elbowroom, for the freedom offered by wide-open spaces. The next time you feel hemmed in by your surroundings, remember that God has promised to lead His faithful ones into a "good and spacious land" (Exodus 3:8 NLT).

❦

THE CITY WAS SHAPED LIKE A CUBE, BECAUSE IT WAS JUST AS HIGH AS IT WAS WIDE. WHEN THE ANGEL MEASURED THE CITY, IT WAS ABOUT FIFTEEN HUNDRED MILES HIGH AND FIFTEEN HUNDRED MILES WIDE.
—REVELATION 21:16 CEV

6.
Big as it is, heaven isn't nearly big enough for God.

Our concept of God is much too small. One day we're going to behold a God who lives both in heaven and beyond. He is far bigger, far greater than we've ever imagined!

King Solomon recognized this. When construction was finished on the magnificent temple he'd built for the Lord, Solomon marveled that the God of the universe intended to dwell within the confines of even so grand a structure. Solomon knew that heaven itself wasn't big enough to encompass God's infinite being. Small wonder that when God's Spirit descended, the glory of the Lord filled the temple!

As we go about our earthly lives, we take little notice of the sun. Whether the day is clear or cloudy, the sun illuminates the world around us. It sustains our very existence by providing the warmth we need, and through photosynthesis and the food chain, the energy we require. But we think of the sun as merely a bright spot in the sky. Children draw a circle with a few squiggly lines and feel they've captured its essence.

To demonstrate the relative size of the earth and the sun, textbooks sometimes illustrate them side by side. In such a picture, the sun appears as a blazing yellow orb too large to portray in its entirety, while the earth is merely a spot on the page. This is an apt image of our face-to-face encounter with the Lord God Almighty, Maker of heaven and earth.

Instead of trying to wrap your mind around the enormity of God—an impossible task—take a step toward heaven by continually breaking down the boundaries with which we all try to confine Him.

❧

"THE HEAVENS, EVEN THE HIGHEST HEAVEN, CANNOT
CONTAIN YOU."
—1 KINGS 8:27

7.
We'll be astounded at how lovely God is.

God is the apex of beauty and love. He is the source and the essence of both, and in Him they rise to meet, become one, and exist together in their purest, truest, highest form. When we behold our Heavenly Father, we won't be able to distinguish between these two qualities; we'll feel His beauty and see His love. God is love, and that's the wonder of His beauty.

The Bible describes God's loveliness in poetic yet earthly terms, using images we can understand to convey a reality we can't. The apostle John likened the Lord's splendor to that of sparkling jewels. In a vision he saw "a Throne set in Heaven with One Seated on the Throne, suffused in gem hues of amber and flame with a nimbus of emerald." (See Revelation 4:2–3 MSG.) To the prophet Ezekiel, God seemed to consist of fire and glowing metal, surrounded by brilliant light. "Brightness everywhere!" he wrote, awestruck by God's glory (Ezekiel 1:28 MSG).

When we enter paradise and experience the magnificence of all the love and grace radiating from God, gone will be all thoughts of golden crowns and heavenly rewards and mansions in glory! We would be content for all eternity just to exist in the presence of such beauty, and feast our eyes upon Him for all time.

Each day, ask the Holy Spirit to help you envision God's beauty and sense His love for you, so that more and more your desire turns to Him alone.

🌿

ONE THING I ASK OF THE LORD, THIS IS WHAT I SEEK: THAT I MAY DWELL IN THE HOUSE OF THE LORD ALL THE DAYS OF MY LIFE, TO GAZE UPON THE BEAUTY OF THE LORD AND TO SEEK HIM IN HIS TEMPLE.
—PSALM 27:4

8.
Jesus' face will shine like an Easter sunrise.

Have you ever watched the sun burst over the horizon on Easter morning? Such beauty leaves no doubt that the heavens indeed declare God's majesty. In paradise we'll have the honor to behold an even lovelier image: the glorified face of Jesus, the same face the disciples saw at the Transfiguration. "Jesus took Peter and the two brothers, James and John, and led them up a high mountain. As the men watched, Jesus' appearance changed so that his face shone like the sun, and his clothing became dazzling white." (See Matthew 17:1–2 NLT.) The radiant face of Christ is one of the most glorious sights in the Bible, and one day we too will witness it!

Jesus briefly revealed His glory on earth to help us understand His true identity. We move closer to heaven the moment we bow before Him and declare, as Peter did, "You are the Messiah, the Son of the living God" (Matthew 16:16 CEV).

❧

HIS FACE WAS LIKE THE SUN SHINING
IN ALL ITS BRILLIANCE.
—REVELATION 1:16

9.
We'll be divinely beautiful.

C. S. Lewis wrote that in heaven each of us will be a "dazzling, radiant, immortal creature, pulsating all through with such energy and joy and wisdom and love as we cannot now imagine." Of course he didn't mean that we will become God, only that we'll finally be perfect reflections of God's image, as we were meant to be from the beginning (Genesis 1:26). Our new bodies will be imperishable, powerful, and glorious (1 Corinthians 15:42–44), like Jesus' resurrected body (Philippians 3:20–21). In fact, the Bible says we'll shine like the sun (Matthew 13:43)!

We all have a desire to be beautiful. The sheer size of the cosmetics industry is testimony to that. Men and women spend an enormous amount of money trying to make themselves look good, buying not only makeup and hair care products but also jewelry, clothes, cars, houses, boats—anything that improves their appearance. Add to that the cost of health food, fitness clubs, and cosmetic surgery, and you get an idea of how deeply we yearn for personal attractiveness. The truth is, all of this merely reflects our longing for love. Imagine not having to work at looking good anymore—just being beautiful! And imagine possessing a beauty that doesn't merely suggest that you are someone worth loving; instead, it flows from you as an outward manifestation of your purity, goodness, and worth. This is the incredible beauty we will enjoy in God's presence. We won't simply look pretty; we'll feel beautiful deep inside ourselves, because our beauty will flow from deep within. And God's eyes will shine upon us. In heaven, we'll be both lovely and loved.

You can take a step closer to this amazing future today by beginning to cultivate your inner beauty, a quality that God greatly values and one that never fades (1 Peter 3:3–4). You become more beautiful inside as you follow Christ and grow to be more and more like Him. The beauty of your spirit is a loveliness you can display here on earth, through your words and deeds, and it is this splendor that you will carry with you into eternity.

❦

THEY'LL BECOME . . . LIKE GEMSTONES IN A CROWN,
CATCHING ALL THE COLORS OF THE SUN.
THEN HOW THEY'LL SHINE! SHIMMER! GLOW!
THE YOUNG MEN ROBUST, THE YOUNG WOMEN LOVELY!
—ZECHARIAH 9:16–17 MSG

10.
We'll have amazing talents.

The Bible talks about the incredible healing that will occur in heaven for those who are physically handicapped on earth. Malachi 4:2 NRSV promises, "For you who revere my name the sun of righteousness shall rise, with healing in its wings." Isaiah 35:5–6 says, "Then will the eyes of the blind be opened and the ears of the deaf unstopped. Then will the lame leap like a deer, and the mute tongue shout for joy."

If you or someone close to you is confined to a wheelchair or suffers from some other physical impairment, these promises are very precious indeed. And the rest of us will be honored and overjoyed to behold the blessed moment of healing and celebration. Surely we'll all rejoice to dance with the lame!

But the truth is, we're all handicapped to some extent in this life. Most of us have far more love in our hearts for God than we're able to express in song and dance. When we consider God's goodness, our spirits soar to heights our voices can't attain, and our love runs so deep that our most graceful attempts at movement can't do it justice.

In heaven we'll all be set free from our physical limitations to fully express our worship and praise.

There we'll be more graceful than any ballerina, and we'll sing like the angels.

Imagine having a voice beautiful enough to extol God's beauty in His very presence, a body graceful enough to celebrate God's grace before His throne. Imagine being able to worship the Lord in a manner worthy to display before Him!

And can you imagine a countless multitude of worshipers, every one of them expressing with unlimited ability, through motion and song, the eternal love, joy, and gratitude in their hearts?

No matter what your limitations in this world may be, find some way to express to God your love for Him, and know that in His eyes you do it beautifully.

🌿

OUR CITIZENSHIP IS IN HEAVEN. AND WE EAGERLY AWAIT A SAVIOR FROM THERE, THE LORD JESUS CHRIST, WHO, BY THE POWER THAT ENABLES HIM TO BRING EVERYTHING UNDER HIS CONTROL, WILL TRANSFORM OUR LOWLY BODIES SO THAT THEY WILL BE LIKE HIS GLORIOUS BODY.
—PHILIPPIANS 3:20–21

11.
Heaven is a premier address.

Just as you have an address that you call home, so does God. Now, you may live on one side of the tracks or the other, but the Lord dwells in the most desirable location in the universe—and beyond! However, God isn't made great because He resides in heaven. The opposite is true: heaven is an amazing, wonderful place because God lives there. His glorious presence is what makes it paradise.

You take a step toward heaven by focusing on God's greatness.

🌱

I LIFT UP MY EYES TO YOU, TO YOU WHOSE THRONE IS
IN HEAVEN.
—PSALM 123:1

12.

God invites everyone to move into His exclusive neighborhood!

Heaven is a very exclusive place—absolutely no sinners allowed. Yet everybody's invited to live there. Through Jesus Christ, God has solved that contradiction. No matter how unworthy we may be, God loves us all and wants us to share His home address with Him for eternity. The Bible says, "The Lord . . . is patient toward you, not wishing for any to perish but for all to come to repentance" (2 Peter 3:9 NASB). Heaven is not just a place where God lives. It's a place where God wants you to live with Him!

When we decide in our hearts that we want to spend eternity with God, we've taken one step closer to heaven.

🌿

GOD HIMSELF SAYS, "I WILL LIVE WITH THESE PEOPLE
AND WALK AMONG THEM."
—2 CORINTHIANS 6:16 CEV

13.
Heaven is a construction zone.

If you could visit heaven right now, you'd have to pardon the dust. God's neighborhood is under construction at the moment, because He's already broken ground on His greatest project ever. You'll want to be there when He cuts the ribbon and unveils His glorious masterpiece of landscape, architecture, and design!

A highlight of the ceremony will be a personal guided tour of the new residence Jesus, the Great Carpenter, is building just for you. Why is God going to all this trouble? He wants you, His child, near Him. God loves you and has planned that His neighborhood will be your new home. He can't get enough of your company because He really does delight in you.

You move closer to heaven when you develop a deep longing for a better place to live (Hebrews 11:16).

JESUS SAID, "IN MY FATHER'S HOUSE ARE MANY ROOMS . . . I AM GOING THERE TO PREPARE A PLACE FOR YOU."
—JOHN 14:2

14.
A flood of blessings awaits us.

In Roald Dahl's book, *Charlie and the Chocolate Factory*, young Charlie Bucket waits excitedly at the gate of Willy Wonka's candy factory, holding his golden ticket, expecting to receive a tour of the facility and a lifetime supply of treats. He can hardly believe it when he later learns that Mr. Wonka intends to give him not only the candy but also the whole factory—with all the wonderful things inside! Like Charlie, we're going to be speechless when we discover all that God has in store for us.

Take a step toward heaven by weighing the cost of following Jesus against all the benefits God is offering.

❧

"SEE IF I WILL NOT THROW OPEN THE FLOODGATES OF HEAVEN AND POUR OUT SO MUCH BLESSING THAT YOU WILL NOT HAVE ROOM ENOUGH FOR IT."
—MALACHI 3:10

15.
Heaven is God's observation post.

It's easy to think that because God lives in heaven and we live on earth, He doesn't know or isn't concerned about what we're going through. But although we can't see God yet, from heaven He sees us. He sees, He understands, and He cares.

When you believe that God is watching you and look up at Him through eyes of faith, you are one step closer to heaven.

❧

THE LORD LOOKS FROM HEAVEN; HE SEES ALL THE
SONS OF MEN. FROM THE PLACE OF HIS DWELLING HE
LOOKS ON ALL THE INHABITANTS OF THE EARTH.
—PSALM 33:13–14 NKJV

16.
We can't reach heaven yet, but our prayers can.

We may not be able to talk with God face-to-face right now, but we can certainly communicate with Him. He listens to us as we pray, telling Him all our joys, sorrows, hopes, and disappointments. He hears our questions and our petitions; and although He doesn't speak to us audibly, He finds ways to respond.

You don't have to be a believer to pray; God will hear your prayers even if you don't know what you believe. If you're unsure whether God exists, pray to Him anyway, asking Him to reveal himself to you if He's real. If you're not a Christian, this is the surest way to take your first step toward heaven.

❦

GOD HEARD THEM, FOR THEIR PRAYER REACHED
HEAVEN, HIS HOLY DWELLING PLACE.
—2 CHRONICLES 30:27

17.
You have a Friend in heaven.

God loves us, even though we are sinners. But God is holy and can't abide the sin in us. As much as He wants us to share His address someday in heaven, as much as He wants to have a relationship with us now, He can do neither as long as our sin is not dealt with. Happily, we have a Friend in heaven, Jesus, who intercedes for us with God (Hebrews 7:24–25). Christ stands as the intermediary between our sinfulness and God's holiness. He is qualified to do this because He is both perfectly holy and perfectly human, and He died to take care of our sins. Because Jesus is our Friend, God can be too.

Every time you confess your sins to Jesus and trust Him to remove them, you've taken a step toward heaven.

🌿

THERE IS SOMEONE IN HEAVEN TO STAND UP FOR ME
AND TAKE MY SIDE.
—JOB 16:19 TEV

18.
There really is a stairway to heaven.

Jacob dreamed of this stairway (Genesis 28:12), which Jesus later revealed to be a vision of himself. If Jacob had lived in more modern times, he might well have seen an escalator, for Christ not only provides access to heaven—which is otherwise unreachable— He provides the power to take us there. The only thing we have to do is step on. We have to place all our trust in Him, committing ourselves completely (it won't do any good to keep one foot on the floor!). But once we put our faith in Jesus, there is no doubt that He will carry us up to our destination.

Jesus said, "I am the way, the truth, and the life. No one comes to the Father except through Me" (John 14:6 NKJV). Believing these words and trusting Jesus to take you to heaven is the biggest step you can take toward getting there. It's the first step onto the stairway to heaven, and it will ensure your salvation.

❦

"I TELL YOU THE TRUTH, YOU SHALL SEE HEAVEN OPEN,
AND THE ANGELS OF GOD ASCENDING AND
DESCENDING ON THE SON OF MAN."
—JOHN 1:51

19.
There's a highway to heaven too.

The Bible gives us another illustration of how we reach paradise. It's not a different way to get there; it's a different picture, another way of thinking about the same process. In this case, instead of a ladder, the image is that of a road, a highway to heaven.

Isaiah 35:8–9 says, "A highway will be there; it will be called the Way of Holiness. The unclean will not journey on it; it will be for those who walk in that Way. . . . Only the redeemed will walk there."

The redeemed are also referred to as "the ransomed of the LORD" (v. 10). Clearly, it's only by God's grace, only through the sacrifice of Jesus on the cross, that we're made worthy to set foot on this highway and begin our journey to paradise. Once we're on the road to heaven, we start to "walk in that Way." What does this mean? God's Word provides some clarification. It says we must "walk in the way of the LORD" (2 Kings 21:22), "walk in the fear of our God" (Nehemiah 5:9), "keep to the paths of the righteous" (Proverbs 2:20), "walk in the way of understanding" (Proverbs 9:6), "walk in the light of the LORD" (Isaiah 2:5), "walk in the footsteps of the faith" (Romans 4:12), and "walk in the truth" (3 John 1:3).

Jesus described the highway to heaven as quite narrow. However, He promised that, unlike the much broader avenue that leads to death, this road leads to life (Matthew 7:13–14). Isaiah 35:10 MSG says, "They'll sing as they make their way home to Zion, unfading halos of joy encircling their heads, welcomed home with gifts of joy and gladness."

How wide is the road you're traveling on? What direction is it headed? If you find you're going the wrong way, ask Jesus to put you on a better course.

❧

THE PATH OF THE RIGHTEOUS IS LIKE THE FIRST GLEAM
OF DAWN, SHINING EVER BRIGHTER TILL THE FULL
LIGHT OF DAY.
—PROVERBS 4:18

20.
There'll be quite a few people there . . .

If it weren't for Jesus, there wouldn't be a single soul in heaven. If it were up to us to get there on our own merit, not one of us would make it. All of us would fall short (Romans 3:23). But—thank God!—that is not the case. Jesus Christ, the Lamb of God, paid the price for our sins (John 1:29). He died on the cross, and because of His sacrifice there will be a countless multitude of people living with God, gratefully praising Him throughout eternity.

Trying to earn your way to heaven is walking in the wrong direction. You'll be a lot closer to where you want to be if you simply stop and turn toward Jesus.

❦

AFTER THIS, I SAW A LARGE CROWD WITH MORE PEOPLE
THAN COULD BE COUNTED. THEY WERE FROM EVERY
RACE, TRIBE, NATION, AND LANGUAGE, AND THEY
STOOD BEFORE THE THRONE AND BEFORE THE LAMB.
—REVELATION 7:9 CEV

21.
. . . And we won't be alone.

Angels are such spectacular beings that we'll be tempted to fall down and worship the first one we see (Revelation 22:8–9). Of course, once we lay eyes on God, we'll be cured of that impulse! However, in heaven we'll meet the great company of the heavenly host that left the shepherds near Bethlehem awestruck as they proclaimed Jesus' birth. We'll see the vast number of angels who shouted for joy as God laid the earth's foundations (Job 38:4–7). And we'll hear them all singing praises to the Lord Jesus Christ. That in itself will be glorious.

Angels are as real as we are. Believing that, and believing everything else the Bible says, will take you one step closer to heaven.

❦

THEN I LOOKED AND HEARD THE VOICE OF MANY
ANGELS, NUMBERING THOUSANDS UPON THOUSANDS,
AND TEN THOUSAND TIMES TEN THOUSAND.
—REVELATION 5:11

22.
We'll work beside the angels.

Angels don't spend all their time singing, and neither will we. God will have work for us to do in heaven, and we will be honored to serve Him right alongside the angels.

God also has work for us to do right now, here on earth. Take a step toward heaven today by dedicating your life to His service.

❧

[THE ANGEL SAID,] "I AM A SERVANT OF GOD,
JUST LIKE YOU."
—REVELATION 22:9 NLT

23.
There's a magnificent rainbow in heaven.

It surrounds God's throne, and it's part of the radiance of His glory.

Whenever you see a rainbow in the sky, let it be a reminder to you not only of God's promise (Genesis 9:12–16) but also of the splendor of His majesty (Ezekiel 1:28).

❧

THERE BEFORE ME WAS A THRONE IN HEAVEN. . . . A RAINBOW, RESEMBLING AN EMERALD, ENCIRCLED THE THRONE.
—REVELATION 4:2–3

24.
There will be no churches in paradise.

God is everywhere; we're always in His presence (Psalm 139:7–10). But here on earth, where we can't see Him, it helps to have a church building serve as the focal point for our worship. In heaven we'll no longer need churches, for God and Jesus will be in plain sight, and they themselves will be our focus.

Brother Lawrence, a seventeenth-century French monk who wrote *Practicing the Presence of God*, taught that we should train ourselves to be more aware of God's presence throughout the day and offer to Him, as an act of worship, every little thing we do. By following this advice, we can be in constant communion with the Lord, and our Sunday morning worship will be all the richer.

Don't wait until Sunday to spend time with God! Take a step toward heaven by worshiping Him all week long, wherever you are.

🌿

I DID NOT SEE A TEMPLE IN THE CITY, BECAUSE ITS TEMPLE IS THE LORD GOD ALMIGHTY AND THE LAMB.
—REVELATION 21:22 TEV

25.
There will be no graveyards, either.

On earth such places are considered hallowed ground, but in paradise they would simply be a waste of good real estate!

We move closer to heaven when we begin to view ourselves as the eternal creatures we really are. If you're a Christian, God has already given you everlasting life. That life doesn't begin when your time on earth ends; it began the moment you accepted Jesus as your Savior. Your spirit is immortal and will never experience death. Jesus has removed the specter of death that once loomed over you, like the sword of Damocles. You have been rescued from the threat of death, liberated from worry and despair, and set free to rejoice.

Whenever you drive past a cemetery, show honor and respect, but let all the crosses you see there remind you of Jesus' promise that in Him you have eternal life, both now and forever.

🌱

"WHOEVER LIVES AND BELIEVES IN ME WILL
NEVER DIE."
—JOHN 11:26

26.
We'll inherit the greatest kingdom in history.

The legend of King Arthur and Camelot inspires nostalgia for a golden age of chivalry, honor, and glory, a time when great strength was employed for the sake of justice and good. This story—about a kingdom that, whether it truly existed or not, lasted but a brief and shining moment—evokes such strong yearnings because there is such a realm, God's kingdom, and we were created to inherit it! The King of heaven desires sons and daughters to be His heirs. And the glory of His kingdom will shine forever.

You step into God's kingdom the moment you declare Jesus Christ as your Lord.

❧

SINCE WE ARE RECEIVING A KINGDOM WHICH CANNOT BE SHAKEN, LET US HAVE GRACE, BY WHICH WE MAY SERVE GOD ACCEPTABLY WITH REVERENCE AND GODLY FEAR.
—HEBREWS 12:28 NKJV

27.
You'll be the toast of heaven.

It's clear that God loves everyone. But do you really believe He loves you individually, personally? If you struggle to believe that you are special, that you have great value in God's sight, He is going to surprise you when you enter heaven. You don't know it, but you are the apple of His eye, and He is going to honor you!

There is a proper, healthy feeling of self-worth that comes when we realize we are deeply loved by our Heavenly Father. You'll feel closer to God's heart, and heaven, if you start believing Him when He tells you, "I've never quit loving you and never will" (Jeremiah 31:3 MSG).

❧

THE LORD TAKES DELIGHT IN HIS PEOPLE; HE
CROWNS THE HUMBLE WITH SALVATION.
—PSALM 149:4

28.
Nothing in heaven will be excellent.

In this world, excellence is all we can hope for. To desire more is simply unrealistic. In heaven, nothing will be excellent. That's not good enough! For our God is not once, not twice, but three times holy (Revelation 4:8), and excellence, however slightly flawed, is not worthy to be found in His presence. Furthermore, He knows that even excellence will never satisfy our deepest yearnings, and He wants to give us only the best. Imagine stepping into paradise and experiencing your first taste of perfection!

Reading the Bible provides us a foretaste of heaven, for, as Psalm 19:7 NASB says, "The law of the LORD is perfect, restoring the soul."

❧

NOTHING IMPURE WILL EVER ENTER IT.
—REVELATION 21:27

29.
There won't be any flies in this ointment.

If God didn't demand perfect holiness of everyone He admitted into His eternal dwelling, it wouldn't be heaven for anyone. Imagine how paradise would be ruined if just one person there were slightly greedy, or selfish, or conceited, or bitter.

You can prepare for an eternity in heaven today by asking the Holy Spirit to help you begin to "put off your old self" and "put on the new self, created to be like God in true righteousness and holiness" (Ephesians 4:22, 24).

❦

GOD'S SPIRIT MAKES US LOVING, HAPPY, PEACEFUL, PATIENT, KIND, GOOD, FAITHFUL, GENTLE, AND SELF-CONTROLLED.
—GALATIANS 5:22–23 CEV

30.
At last, no more thistles!

When Adam and Eve sinned, God told them, "Cursed is the ground for your sake; in toil you shall eat *of it* all the days of your life. Both thorns and thistles it shall bring forth for you" (Genesis 3:17–18 NKJV). Now, there had been work to do in the perfect environment of Eden before the Fall, in caring for God's garden. It was only afterward that this joyful toil turned painful. Have you ever worked on a project, however pleasant, that didn't involve some frustration? We start out happily whistling, and sooner or later we're angrily muttering. Imagine how enjoyable and satisfying it will be to put in a good day's work in paradise without pricking your finger on a single thorn!

Ask God to help you graciously endure life's little annoyances until you're with Him in heaven and they are no more.

NO LONGER WILL THERE BE ANY CURSE.
—REVELATION 22:3

31.
It might be hard to get some sleep.

Bathed in the splendor of God's glory, surrounded by all the wonder and excitement of heaven, we might find it hard to get some shut-eye. Then again, we probably won't want to sleep much. Maybe we won't have to at all!

Psalm 63:6 says, "On my bed I remember you; I think of you through the watches of the night." During those nights when you can't sleep, spend time praying to God and contemplating the mysteries of heaven.

❧

THERE WILL BE NO NIGHT THERE—NO NEED FOR LAMPS OR SUN—FOR THE LORD GOD WILL SHINE ON THEM.
—REVELATION 22:5 NLT

32.
Time will be irrelevant.

Time flies far too quickly here on earth. How often have you experienced a perfect moment and thought, *I wish this would never end!* Perhaps you were on the golf course with good friends on a beautiful summer evening. The sun was just beginning to set, the temperature was perfect, and you were thoroughly enjoying the fresh air, the light exercise, the friendly competition, and the great camaraderie. But before you knew it, you were standing on the eighteenth green in the twilight, watching the last putt drop, shaking hands and saying good-bye. Or perhaps you were sitting in the coffee shop catching up with a family member who lives out of state. The espresso's aroma created a warm, pleasant atmosphere, and your dessert was fantastic. It was just the two of you, and there was so much to discuss! It felt so good to reconnect, so wonderful just to be together again. You could have talked all night. But soon the store owner was changing the sign on the door, and you knew it was time to leave.

Life's perfect moments have one flaw: they are over long before we want them to be. Not so in heaven! There we will be able to savor each perfect moment, basking in each glorious experience, until our heart is full and the Lord invites us to the next.

When you find yourself wishing that time would stand still, take a step toward heaven by praising God for the moment and thanking Him that someday, in paradise, it will.

🌱

WITH THE LORD A DAY IS LIKE A THOUSAND YEARS,
AND A THOUSAND YEARS ARE LIKE A DAY.
—2 PETER 3:8

33.
Dictionaries will be much thinner.

Throughout the dictionary, there are countless words for which we will no longer have any use in paradise, words such as anger, betrayal, corruption, deceit, envy, failure, guilt, heartache, illness . . .

Many of these words we are forced to live with in this world. But many of them you can start crossing out of your dictionary today, if you begin to live by the power of the Holy Spirit within you. These words are deleted as you turn away from sin, and every time you get rid of one, you take a step closer to heaven.

❧

THERE WILL BE NO MORE DEATH, NO MORE GRIEF OR
CRYING OR PAIN.
—REVELATION 21:4 TEV

34.
There will be no time for good-byes.

In 1965 the Byrds' song "Turn, Turn, Turn" introduced many people to the words of Ecclesiastes 3:1–8 NKJV, which begins, "To everything *there is* a season, a time for every purpose under heaven. . . . " The song may be timeless, but its message, though based on God's Word, is not eternal.

That little phrase under heaven means that these words apply only to life on earth. In heaven the passage will be only half true! Though we have all eternity, there will be no time for dying, uprooting, killing, tearing down, weeping, mourning, scattering, refraining, giving up, throwing away, rending, silence, hatred, or war. We'll be too busy living and planting and healing and building and laughing and dancing and gathering and embracing and searching and keeping and mending and speaking and loving and enjoying sweet, everlasting peace!

The time for reunions will have arrived, the time for rejoining loved ones. It will be a time of reconnecting and rejoicing, unencumbered by the specter of sin and sorrow. And there will never again come a time for farewells.

If there's a rift in one of your relationships, perhaps the time for healing and embracing is now.

❧

GLADNESS AND JOY WILL OVERTAKE THEM, AND
SORROW AND SIGHING WILL FLEE AWAY.
—ISAIAH 35:10

35.
Our "daily walk with the Lord" will have new meaning.

Imagine the joy that Adam and Eve knew in paradise. They had perfect fellowship with God! Each day they strolled with Him through the Garden of Eden, savoring His companionship.

The amazing thing is, God loved their company as much as they loved His. He valued His relationship with them so much, in fact, that even before it was severed by their sin, He made plans to restore it. And because of His determination, because He was willing to pay the ultimate price by sacrificing His only Son, we all have the opportunity, if we choose, to walk with God, joyfully relishing His presence—in spirit here on earth, and in person one fine day in heaven.

We sometimes think of our walk with the Lord as a daily grind, reducing it to nothing more than trying to avoid temptation and do the right thing. But we must not miss the significance of our privilege to walk with God!

In the genealogy of Genesis 5, only basic facts are given for most of the people listed. However, special mention is made of two men, Enoch and Noah. The Bible makes a point of saying that both of them walked with the Lord (Genesis 5:24; 6:9). Exodus

33:11 defines more clearly the nature of their relationship with God: "The LORD would speak to Moses face to face, as a man speaks with his friend."

Don't follow Jesus from a distance! Move up closer and enjoy His company. We follow Christ best when we're walking right beside Him, talking with Him all along our journey.

❧

THEY HEARD THE SOUND OF THE LORD GOD WALKING IN THE GARDEN IN THE COOL OF THE DAY.
—GENESIS 3:8 NKJV

36.
We'll enjoy God's best.

The master of the wedding banquet in Cana was the first to taste the water that Jesus turned into wine (John 2:1–11). Not knowing what had just transpired, he marveled at its quality and asked the bridegroom why he hadn't served the best, choicest wine first!

At that point in the celebration, well into the festivities, a low-grade wine would have sufficed. The guests, in high spirits from the wine they'd already consumed, probably wouldn't have noticed the difference. But when God wants to bless His children, He doesn't do it halfway. He pulls out all the stops. The Bible says there is not one good thing that He will withhold from us (Psalm 84:11). In heaven we'll enjoy the utmost God has to offer—the crème de la crème of all His wonders!

Think of the best meal you've ever eaten. What made it so special? Was it the exquisite food, the fine drink, the wonderful ambiance, the lovely music, the charming company? The marvelous banquet God is planning for His children in heaven will feature only the first-rate, the top of the line in every category.

God wants to give us His very best because He loves us so much. It will bring Him great pleasure to lavishly and extravagantly bless us with one perfect delight after another.

We can begin to enjoy God's best today. He's ready, willing, and able to freely satisfy our spiritual hunger and thirst. In Isaiah 55:1–2 MSG God invites us all to come to Him, saying, "Listen to me, listen well: Eat only the best, fill yourself with only the finest."

🌿

ON THIS MOUNTAIN THE LORD ALMIGHTY WILL PRE-PARE A FEAST OF RICH FOOD FOR ALL PEOPLES, A BAN-QUET OF AGED WINE—THE BEST OF MEATS AND THE FINEST OF WINES.
—ISAIAH 25:6

37.
We'll be welcome at God's throne.

John F. Kennedy used to allow his children to play under his desk in the Oval Office, even as he conducted the affairs of the nation. Only the children of the president could ever enjoy such a prerogative! God also loves to have His children nearby, and although He is Lord Almighty, Ruler of heaven and earth, He is most delighted when we know and relate to Him intimately as Father. In heaven we will forever be honored to play at His feet.

Through Jesus you are truly God's child (1 John 3:1), and through prayer you can take full advantage even now of your wonderful privilege to "approach the throne of grace with confidence" (Hebrews 4:16).

❧

EVERYONE WHO WINS THE VICTORY WILL SIT WITH ME
ON MY THRONE.
—REVELATION 3:21 CEV

38.
Everything in heaven will be brand-spanking new.

King Solomon once groused, "There is nothing new under the sun" (Ecclesiastes 1:9 NRSV). But he'll have no cause to complain in eternity. Not only will God create a new heaven and a new earth, such that we'll marvel forever at His innovative genius, but He'll also institute a new order (Revelation 21:1–4). There'll be a lot of new things, and a whole new way of doing things!

There's going to be a whole new you, as well. In fact, God has already begun His makeover of you. Second Corinthians 5:17 NLT says, "Those who become Christians become new persons. They are not the same anymore, for the old life is gone. A new life has begun!" By the time you enter heaven, God will have completed His work in you, and like the rest of paradise, you'll be perfect—all shining and new.

What will this new you be like? You'll be free from sin (Romans 6:6–7), you'll have a new attitude and be truly righteous and holy (Ephesians 4:22–24), and you'll be clothed with compassion, kindness, humility, gentleness, patience, and love (Colossians 3:12–14). That's quite a makeover—and quite a wardrobe! The new you will fit right into God's brand-new, flawless environment, for just as the old, sinful you will cease to exist, in heaven "the old order of things has passed away" (Revelation 21:4).

We can cooperate with God here on earth and be that much closer to heaven, ready for eternity, by spending time in the Scriptures each day and allowing the Holy Spirit to renew our hearts and minds.

🌱

HE WHO WAS SEATED ON THE THRONE SAID, "I AM MAKING EVERYTHING NEW!"
—REVELATION 21:5

39.
There will be endless wonders to explore.

Psalm 139 says there are no limits to God's creative mind. And His unlimited power gives Him the ability to make all His thoughts into reality. How blessed we will be to probe the fathomless depths of eternity!

It will take us all of forever to explore heaven, and just as long to comprehend the mind of our Heavenly Father. But God has made it possible for us to start knowing Him today, by providing us with the Bible, the church, the world around us, and most of all His Holy Spirit, through whom we experience the presence of our Creator.

🌿

O LORD MY GOD, YOU HAVE DONE MANY MIRACLES
FOR US. YOUR PLANS FOR US ARE TOO NUMEROUS TO
LIST. IF I TRIED TO RECITE ALL YOUR WONDERFUL
DEEDS, I WOULD NEVER COME TO THE END OF THEM.
—PSALM 40:5 NLT

40.
We'll discover what true riches really are.

Jesus said that if we proved we could be faithful with worldly wealth, God would know He could trust us with true riches (Luke 16:10–12). One of the thrills of heaven will be to behold the wealth that God considers to have superior worth and everlasting value.

When children are learning about money, they often have a hard time understanding that a dime is worth more than a nickel. Dimes are smaller, thinner, and weigh less than nickels. How can they be worth more? A child has to take it on faith that Mom and Dad know which coin is more valuable. In the same way, we must trust God's wisdom as we make choices about which things in life hold the most worth.

God says the true riches of heaven far outweigh those of this world. What will these treasures turn out to be? Will they consist of physical items, such as precious metals and gemstones more beautiful than we can imagine? Or are God's riches composed of spiritual blessings, such as the fruit and gifts of the Spirit mentioned in the Bible? Perhaps the true riches are more relational in nature, that is, the eternal fellowship we will cherish with God and enjoy with one another. Or it could be that this incredible treasure is nothing less than the immeasurable, incomprehensible love of Christ (Ephesians 3:17–19).

Whatever these eternal riches turn out to be (and maybe it's all of the above!), God has ordained that all of them are to be found through a relationship with His Son, Jesus.

While we ponder such questions and wait, it's good to reflect on Proverbs 16:16 NRSV, which says, "How much better to get wisdom than gold! To get understanding is to be chosen rather than silver." Just as worldly wealth is surpassed by God's treasures in heaven, so it is eclipsed by God's wisdom here on earth.

Pursuing wisdom instead of money in this life will lead you closer to the true riches.

🌿

MY PURPOSE IS THAT THEY MAY BE ENCOURAGED IN HEART AND UNITED IN LOVE, SO THAT THEY MAY HAVE THE FULL RICHES OF COMPLETE UNDERSTANDING, IN ORDER THAT THEY MAY KNOW THE MYSTERY OF GOD, NAMELY, CHRIST, IN WHOM ARE HIDDEN ALL THE TREASURES OF WISDOM AND KNOWLEDGE.
—COLOSSIANS 2:2–3

41.
We'll eat the ultimate health food.

The health food business would be revolutionized if just one company could package and sell fruit from the Tree of Life. God himself said that if anyone eats this produce, they will live forever. How much healthier can a food be?

There's bad news for the health food industry, because this tree can be found in only two places: the Garden of Eden and heaven. But there's good news for consumers, for God has made it possible for everyone to gain access to heaven and its life-giving fruit and offers it to us all free of charge.

In heaven we'll enjoy the taste and benefits of heaven's fruit. Here on earth God provides us with spiritual food that is equally delicious, found in the Bible. Psalm 119:103 says, "How sweet are your words to my taste, sweeter than honey to my mouth!" God's Word, consumed regularly, will assure your spiritual health until you enter eternity.

❧

"TO THOSE WHO WIN THE VICTORY I WILL GIVE THE
RIGHT TO EAT THE FRUIT OF THE TREE OF LIFE THAT
GROWS IN THE GARDEN OF GOD."
—REVELATION 2:7 TEV

42.
We'll drink the purest of waters.

Companies that sell water in plastic bottles would go out of business in heaven. The most expensive premium bottled water can't compare with the pure, life-giving water flowing from the river of the water of life. This river is crystal-clear and flows from God's throne right through the heart of the eternal city (Revelation 22:1–2).

Again, there's good news for consumers: heaven's H_2O, like its fruit, is absolutely free to anyone who desires it!

You don't have to wait for heaven to quench your spiritual thirst. Ask Jesus for living water today; He promised to give it to all who come to Him (John 4:10–14), and it will satisfy you.

❧

THE SPIRIT AND THE BRIDE SAY, "COME!" AND LET HIM WHO HEARS SAY, "COME!" WHOEVER IS THIRSTY, LET HIM COME; AND WHOEVER WISHES, LET HIM TAKE THE FREE GIFT OF THE WATER OF LIFE.
—REVELATION 22:17

43.
We'll learn the rest of the story.

God has been writing an epoch story, the proportions of which extend far beyond our imagination. Only a fraction of it has been recorded in the Bible. In heaven we'll be privileged to hear it narrated by the Author himself. Imagine the master Storyteller mesmerizing us with chapter after chapter of His grand saga, full of romance, drama, comedy, and adventure, and alive with richly drawn characters facing tremendous challenges, making choices with life-altering consequences—and all of it true!

We'll cheer and applaud for the subject of each chapter as the Lord graciously bids him or her to rise and be recognized. Best of all, we'll learn about all the marvelous, untold things God's Son, Jesus, has done since the dawn of time—and we'll love Him even more. Then finally, when the whole wonderful, heart-lifting tale is finished, like happy children we'll beg our Father to tell it again and again.

Even on your most ho-hum, bland, ordinary day, God is vigorously at work in the world, by His Spirit, through His church, in the hearts and lives of people everywhere! He is worthy to be praised for what He has done, what He is doing today, and what He will do from now through eternity.

🌿

JESUS DID MANY OTHER THINGS AS WELL. IF EVERY ONE OF THEM WERE WRITTEN DOWN, I SUPPOSE THAT EVEN THE WHOLE WORLD WOULD NOT HAVE ROOM FOR THE BOOKS THAT WOULD BE WRITTEN.
—JOHN 21:25

44.
Heaven has more animals than the Jungle Book.

Children sometimes wonder if there will be animals in heaven. Adults sometimes wonder if there will be children.

The Bible makes it very clear that there will be both. Jesus said, "Let the children alone, and do not hinder them from coming to Me; for the kingdom of heaven belongs to such as these" (Matthew 19:14 NASB). And just one small passage in the book of Isaiah mentions ten different kinds of animals in heaven. There are wolves and lambs and leopards and goats and lions and deer and cows and bears and oxen and snakes (Isaiah 11:6–8). Snakes in heaven—now, there's an amazing fact!

In paradise, however, it will be God's law, not the law of the jungle. People and animals will live with each other peacefully, harmoniously. Lions will eat straw, and even the snakes will be harmless. Yes, there are animals in heaven. Children too. Kids will probably be chasing frogs throughout eternity, and it will be difficult to tell which are happier.

The Bible says it's very good and pleasant when people live together in unity (Psalm 133:1). You'll experience a piece of heaven on earth if you always do your best to live at peace with everyone (Romans 12:18).

❧

IN THAT DAY THE WOLF AND THE LAMB WILL LIVE TOGETHER; THE LEOPARD AND THE GOAT WILL BE AT PEACE. CALVES AND YEARLINGS WILL BE SAFE AMONG LIONS, AND A LITTLE CHILD WILL LEAD THEM ALL.
—ISAIAH 11:6 NLT

45.
We'll hear the real Hallelujah Chorus.

Perhaps the great composer himself, George Frideric Handel, will conduct all the angels and saints as we sing. Perhaps the King of Kings will stand to honor the moment. Could it be that all the music of heaven will have been written here on earth?

We were created to worship God, and we take a step toward heaven as we join with the angels and saints even now in lifting up our earthly voices to praise Him.

🍃

I HEARD AS IT WERE THE VOICE OF A GREAT MULTI-TUDE, AND AS THE VOICE OF MANY WATERS, AND AS THE VOICE OF MIGHTY THUNDERINGS, SAYING, ALLELUIA: FOR THE LORD GOD OMNIPOTENT REIGNETH.
—REVELATION 19:6 KJV

46.
God's going to give us a crown . . .

A crown is much like a trophy or an award. Even if it were quite valuable, crafted of pure, solid gold or fine crystal and studded with jewels, it wouldn't have much meaning if we simply made it for ourselves. However, when the King of Kings stands before you and places a priceless crown upon your head, rewarding you for your faithfulness, that will be a moment of utmost significance and honor!

On our journey to heaven, the apostle Paul advises us, "Run in such a way as to get the prize. Everyone who competes in the games goes into strict training. They do it to get a crown that will not last; but we do it to get a crown that will last forever" (1 Corinthians 9:24–25).

🌱

I HAVE FOUGHT THE GOOD FIGHT, I HAVE FINISHED THE RACE, I HAVE KEPT THE FAITH. NOW THERE IS IN STORE FOR ME THE CROWN OF RIGHTEOUSNESS, WHICH THE LORD, THE RIGHTEOUS JUDGE, WILL AWARD TO ME ON THAT DAY—AND NOT ONLY TO ME, BUT ALSO TO ALL WHO HAVE LONGED FOR HIS APPEARING.
—2 TIMOTHY 4:7–8

47.
. . . And we'll give it right back.

In that sublime moment when the Lord is honoring you and presenting you to receive the praise of heaven, you will look up into His loving eyes and know in your heart the truth of the matter. And like the twenty-four elders who surround God's throne (Revelation 4:4), you'll remove the crown from your head, kneel before God, and worshipfully place it at His feet, as if to say, "No, Lord. You deserve the praise. I couldn't have done it without You." Before the multitudes of heaven you will give Him the glory for all He has done in your life.

Just as it is here on earth, in heaven we'll be able to offer to God only what He's already given to us. We can't add to God's infinite glory; all we can do is reflect it back to Him.

When you receive honor and praise for your achievements in this world, don't hesitate to give God all the glory. You may be tempted to give Him only partial credit, feeling you accomplished something worthwhile with a little help from above, but in fact God created you, gifted you with talents and abilities, molded you through your circumstances, education, and experience, arranged every opportunity, and empowered you even as you worked. He chose you for His wonderful purposes, and He made it possible for you to fulfill them. Stand back and give Him the limelight He deserves, and be thankful that He allowed you to be part of it all.

❧

THEY PLACED THEIR CROWNS IN FRONT OF THE THRONE AND SAID, "OUR LORD AND GOD, YOU ARE WORTHY TO RECEIVE GLORY, HONOR, AND POWER. YOU CREATED ALL THINGS, AND BY YOUR DECISION THEY ARE AND WERE CREATED."
—REVELATION 4:10–11 CEV

48.
Christmas will be glorious!

Did you ever consider that God might have created evergreens just because He knew that we, living in a world often dark and dreary, would need the hope offered by the tiny splendor of a Christmas tree? When God commanded, "Let there be light," was He, in some corner of His infinite mind, already envisioning the modest glory of a Northern pine all decorated and radiant in honor of the incarnation of His Son?

Our God is a God of celebration. After He delivered the Israelites from slavery in Egypt, He commanded them to set aside certain days of the year as holy days, on which sacred feasts would be held to recall the wonderful things He'd done for them. These religious festivals included symbolic traditions, holy fellowship, acts of worship, and displays of happiness and joy. Our Heavenly Father created holidays, and He loves to celebrate them with us!

Whether Christmas in heaven is observed periodically or continually, whether it is rung in with earth's traditions or in ways we can't imagine, the commemoration of the miracle of Jesus' birth—and the many blessings it has brought to humankind—is sure to be an incredible part of our eternal life with Him.

We move closer to heaven when we keep our focus on Jesus during the holidays and throughout the year.

❧

FOR TO US A CHILD IS BORN, TO US A SON IS GIVEN,
AND THE GOVERNMENT WILL BE ON HIS SHOULDERS.
AND HE WILL BE CALLED WONDERFUL COUNSELOR,
MIGHTY GOD, EVERLASTING FATHER,
PRINCE OF PEACE.
—ISAIAH 9:6

49.
God will be proud of us . . .

In their book *The Blessing*, Gary Smalley and John Trent write, "All of us long to be accepted by others. . . . This yearning is especially true in our relationship with our parents. . . . For sons or daughters in biblical times, receiving their father's blessing was a momentous event. . . . It gave these children a tremendous sense of being highly valued."

The blessing that a father gives his child is a reflection of the blessing our Heavenly Father desires to bestow on us, and one day will. God loves each of us deeply, and He wants us to know how proud He is of us, how happy He is that we belong to Him. He longs to hold us and commend us with words of praise and affirmation.

If you are in Christ Jesus, when you reach heaven you will stand in God's presence, feel Him put His arm around your shoulders, and hear Him say—just as Jesus heard Him say on the day He was baptized— "You are My beloved [child], in whom I am well pleased" (Mark 1:11 NKJV).

We take a step toward heaven when we realize that God's love for Jesus flows through His Son and to us, if we remain in Christ like branches on the Vine

(John 15:5).

You don't have to wait for heaven to begin hearing God's words of acceptance, approval, and love. Listen carefully for the whisper of His voice, for as Romans 8:16 says, "The Spirit himself testifies with our spirit that we are God's children."

❧

GOD IS NOT ASHAMED FOR THEM TO CALL HIM
THEIR GOD.
—HEBREWS 11:16 TEV

50.
. . . And Jesus will be too.

The day you step into eternity, Jesus will embrace you as well, saying, "You truly are a member of the family of God." For long ago He promised, "Everyone . . . who acknowledges me before others, I also will acknowledge before my Father in heaven" (Matthew 10:32 NRSV).

Stop for a moment and consider the great love of Jesus. He loves you so much that He was willing to die for you, even though He was completely aware of the sinful things you have done. He's not disappointed in you for the wrongs you've confessed to Him; He's glad you came to Him so He could wipe the slate clean. Stay near to Him. The closer you remain to Jesus, the more confident you'll be in His love for you, and the closer you'll feel to heaven.

❧

JESUS IS NOT ASHAMED TO CALL THEM BROTHERS.
—HEBREWS 2:11

51.
The Lord will reward us for every kindness we've ever shown Him.

In the classic novel *Great Expectations*, the central character, a poor orphan named Pip, is shocked to discover that his mysterious benefactor is not the wealthy Miss Havisham, as he'd always believed. Instead, it is a man he met long ago when he was a boy. The man was a desperate escaped convict to whom Pip had brought some food. Years later this man, who by that time was earning an honest living, and who'd always remembered Pip's kindness, had begun giving Pip money anonymously to help him get established in life.

Jesus, too, remembers every gracious act shown Him. But how can we do anything for the Son of God? Christ taught that each time we reach out to someone in need, we do Him a valuable service. He said, "Whatever you did for one of the least of these brothers of mine, you did for me" (Matthew 25:40). To those who minister to Him this way, our Lord will one day say in heaven, "I was hungry and you gave me something to eat, I was thirsty and you gave me something to drink, I was a stranger and you invited me in, I needed clothes and you clothed me, I was sick and you looked after me, I was in prison and you came to visit me" (Matthew 25:34–36). Can you imagine hearing gratitude in the voice of the Lord?

And what is the reward for a cup of water? What is the compensation for a piece of bread? What should one get in exchange for a night's shelter, an article of clothing, some comfort, a little companionship?
Pip received the financial blessings of an earthly benefactor. The riches our heavenly Benefactor will bestow upon us will last throughout eternity. In God's economy, a cup of water merits a kingdom.

The Bible says the kind of faith that pleases God involves looking after people in distress (James 1:27). We move closer to heaven when we begin seeing Jesus in the face of the downtrodden, caring for these people He loves, and thereby serving Him in spirit here on earth, just as we will in person there.

❧

"COME, YOU BLESSED OF MY FATHER, INHERIT THE
KINGDOM PREPARED FOR YOU FROM THE FOUNDATION
OF THE WORLD."
—MATTHEW 25:34 NKJV

52.
We'll never know darkness again.

There's a dark side to everyone's character, but not to God's. Sin is present in us, but not in Him. And heaven, God's home, is free from any trace of evil, for He will never allow anything impure to come into His presence (Revelation 21:27). That's why, before we can enter paradise, Christ must purify us from all sin.

In heaven our existence will be completely unlike the life we experienced on earth. There will be no sin in us, and no sin around us. We'll be free from the temptation to commit evil and the threat of being harmed by evil. The only thing we'll know is the light of God's glory and goodness! And finally our own character will fully reflect His.

Sadly, this world is steeped in darkness. Yet Jesus said, "I am the light of the world. If you follow me, you won't be stumbling through the darkness, because you will have the light that leads to life" (John 8:12 NLT). We move closer to heaven when we see this light and begin to walk in it.

❧

GOD IS LIGHT, PURE LIGHT; THERE'S NOT A TRACE OF
DARKNESS IN HIM.
—1 JOHN 1:5 MSG

53.
We'll discover that God is the most cheerful giver of all.

God gave us Jesus, His only Son, so we could have eternal life (John 3:16). This one gift revealed the extent of God's love for us, because it involved God giving up what was most precious to Him. Since He was willing to do that, we know there's nothing He won't do for us. Romans 8:32 says, "He who did not spare his own Son, but gave him up for us all—how will he not also, along with him, graciously give us all things?"

What's amazing is, making such a painful sacrifice as allowing Jesus to be nailed to the cross has ultimately brought great joy to God. And continuing to give to us so freely and abundantly in this life goes on bringing Him joy. God is a generous lover, and He's looking forward to having us all with Him in heaven, where for all eternity He can bless us to His heart's content.

The Lord wants us to reflect His lavish, extravagant nature. Second Corinthians 9:7 NKJV says, "God loves a cheerful giver." It may well be that in heaven, but to a much greater extent than on earth, we will both receive blessings from God and pass along those blessings to one another. Take a step toward that glorious future by serving and giving to others lovingly and cheerfully today.

❧

"YOUR FATHER HAS BEEN PLEASED TO GIVE YOU THE KINGDOM."
—LUKE 12:32

54.
Every i will be dotted . . .

In God's grand design for history and eternity, no detail will be overlooked. In the Hebrew alphabet, a "jot" is the littlest letter, similar to an apostrophe, and a "tittle" is a tiny mark used to indicate accent.

Jesus declared, in essence, that every dot and dash in God's Word is there for a reason, and by the time we all get to heaven each of God's purposes will be completed to the letter, even to the punctuation mark. One day we'll both be honored and awestruck to witness the absolute fulfillment of God's great plan.

🌱

JESUS SAID, "TILL HEAVEN AND EARTH PASS AWAY, ONE JOT OR ONE TITTLE WILL BY NO MEANS PASS FROM THE LAW TILL ALL IS FULFILLED."
—MATTHEW 5:18 NKJV

55.
. . . Every t crossed.

The New International Version of the Bible translates *jot* as "the smallest letter," and *tittle* as "the least stroke a pen." Think about God's plan for your life. Every jot and tittle will be fulfilled there as well. On a day when it seems like you're losing your struggle against sin and discouragement, remember that God will accomplish His purpose for you.

God to Him and throw yourself on His mercy. Watch how He moves in your heart and life to help you fight that battle. He promises power over sin in His Word. So trust in His truth. You take a step toward heaven when you put your trust in all of God's Word.

❧

THE RAIN AND SNOW COME DOWN FROM THE HEAVENS AND STAY ON THE GROUND TO WATER THE EARTH. THEY CAUSE THE GRAIN TO GROW, PRODUCING SEED FOR THE FARMER AND BREAD FOR THE HUNGRY. IT IS THE SAME WITH MY WORD. I SEND IT OUT, AND IT ALWAYS PRODUCES FRUIT. IT WILL ACCOMPLISH ALL I WANT IT TO, AND IT WILL PROSPER EVERYWHERE I SEND IT.
—ISAIAH 55:10–11 NLT

56.
Jesus rules in heaven . . .

Jesus is the King of heaven. God has given Him the authority to make decisions and the power to uphold them. His reign will never end. And the King of heaven wants you as His friend and close companion for all eternity.

We take a step toward heaven by accepting Jesus not only as our Savior but also as our King.

🌿

JESUS CAME UP AND SPOKE TO THEM, SAYING, "ALL AUTHORITY HAS BEEN GIVEN TO ME IN HEAVEN AND ON EARTH."
—MATTHEW 28:18 NASB

57.
. . . And we'll reign with Him.

Christ will relegate some of His power and authority in heaven to us. He won't give it away, and we will never be His equals; we'll continue to worship and obey Him forever (Daniel 7:27). But we will be given the honor and responsibility to rule under His command.

The disciples often argued over which of them would be the greatest in the kingdom of heaven. Jesus said that whoever wanted to be first must put himself last and serve everyone else (Mark 9:33–35). If you're in a position of authority here on earth, move closer to heaven by being a servant leader, as Jesus was (Mark 10:45).

❧

IF WE ENDURE, WE WILL ALSO REIGN WITH HIM.
—2 TIMOTHY 2:12

58.
We'll be even greater than the angels.

Angels are magnificent, powerful beings, but God will place them all under our authority.

Never fall into the temptation to worship angels (Revelation 22:8–9). Keep your focus on God, and worship Him instead.

🌱

DON'T YOU KNOW THAT WE WILL JUDGE ANGELS?
—1 CORINTHIANS 6:3 CEV

59.
Paradise will bear God's handprints—and our fingerprints.

J. R. R. Tolkien, a man of faith who authored *The Hobbit* and *The Lord of the Rings*, suggested in his writings that each of us, as "sub-creators" made in the image of the Creator, will have the opportunity to add our own personal touch to heaven, expressing with our God-given talents and abilities the creativity the Lord has woven into our very nature.

This belief makes sense, as this is the way God chose to work when He formed the earth. Have you ever visited a lovely botanical garden? Consider the way God produces such a wonderful setting. First, He creates an incredible variety of trees, shrubs, flowers, and grasses. Then, He provides rocks and water and other raw materials. Finally, He steps back and allows us, the people He created and endowed with imagination, intelligence, and skill, to artistically arrange all these elements, crafting a place of beauty, serenity, and inspiration—a garden that ultimately reflects God's glory. Surely the Lord would not give us such passion and ability to create, just to leave our hands idle for all eternity!

Putting your God-given talents to work here on earth to make the world a more beautiful place and glorify God will give you a deep sense of fulfillment and take you one step closer to heaven.

🌱

THE LORD GOD TOOK THE MAN AND PUT
HIM IN THE GARDEN OF EDEN TO WORK IT AND
TAKE CARE OF IT.
—GENESIS 2:15

60.
We'll rejoice forever that all God's children are home.

A man was sitting with his seven-year-old son on the boy's bed one night, just before bedtime. "What story would you like me to read tonight?" the father asked. His son surprised him by saying, "Tell me one instead." Not at all adept at making up stories on the spur of the moment, the man searched his memory for a good tale. Finally he said, "Would you like to hear the one about the prodigal son, from the Bible?" His son agreed, having never heard it before. So the man began telling the story in his own words, as dramatically as he could, hoping he'd remember all the details.

"Once there was a young man," he began, "who decided he didn't want to live with his father anymore. He didn't like all the work he had to do. He didn't like having to follow his father's rules all the time. He wanted to go out and see the world. He was looking for fun and adventure. He just wanted to enjoy life."

His son was listening attentively.

"So he went up to his father one day and asked for his half of his father's money. You see, he had a brother, and he knew that when his father died, he and his brother would each get half of their dad's money.

"Now, this request made his father very sad, because it was just as if the young man had said to him, 'I wish you were already dead.' But the father gave the young man the money he wanted and let him go away.

"The young man traveled to a faraway country, where for a while he had a great time, eating and drinking and dancing and having fun with all his new friends. He spent a bunch of money. But then do you know what happened?"

"He ran out of money?"

"That's right. Pretty soon all the money was gone. He'd spent it all. Then he had no money for food and no place to live. All of his friends went away when they saw he was broke. So he got a job. It wasn't a very good one, but it was the only job he could find. He had to feed a farmer's pigs. It was dirty, smelly work, but he didn't have much choice. He didn't have any money and he was hungry.

"He didn't earn a lot feeding pigs, so he wasn't able to buy much food. Soon he got so hungry that he started wishing he could eat the pigs' food!"

His son made a face, and they both laughed. "Then one day he had an idea. He decided to go home. He knew he'd done a lot of bad things. He'd hurt his father's feelings very badly. He didn't think he deserved to be treated like a son anymore, but he thought that if he begged his father, maybe he'd let him be like one of the servants at home. He figured those servants were better off than he was now. At least they had enough food to eat.

"So he traveled back to his father's house. And do

you know what he saw when he looked way up the road on the way?"

"What?"

"His dad was waiting for him there on the road. He didn't know it, but his father had been waiting there a long time. The young man was scared. He didn't know what his father was going to say. He was sure his dad was still angry. So he kept practicing what he was going to say to his father, how he was going to apologize and ask to be treated like a servant from now on.

"But then he saw his dad start running toward him! When he got to him, his father grabbed him and gave him a huge bear hug. The whole time the young man was trying to say, 'I'm sorry, Father. I don't deserve to be your son. Can I be a servant instead?' But his father wasn't even listening. He called for his servants to get a big party ready. Then he hugged the young man again and said, 'Son, I'm so glad you're home. Let's go celebrate!'"

When the man finished the story, he was surprised to see tears in his son's eyes. The boy was moved by this father's love. "Why didn't his dad punish him for being so bad?" he wondered.

His father told him, "It's because he knew his son had already learned his lesson. All he had to do was come home."

The boy thought about this for a moment. Then he asked, "If I was bad and ran away, would you wait for me? Would you run to me?"

Now there were tears in the man's eyes as well. "I'd wait just as long as he did. I'd run even faster. And I'd throw you the biggest party you ever saw!"

There is something about a father's love that touches every heart. It will be the same in heaven. Each time we see the Father surrounded by all His lost children come home, and behold the love in His face, our own eyes will fill with tears of joy, the celebration will begin anew, and once again we'll dance with the angels in the golden streets.

One of the first steps we take toward heaven is when we come to our senses and begin to yearn for home.

❧

"THERE IS JOY IN THE PRESENCE OF THE ANGELS OF GOD OVER ONE SINNER WHO REPENTS."
—LUKE 15:10 NKJV

61.
God will never grow tired of us . . .

Family reunions are great, but invariably there comes a time when, as much as we love our relatives, they start to annoy us. We begin to look forward to seeing them leave. However, God will never grow weary of our company. He'll never wish our time in heaven with Him would end. And—wonder of wonders—we'll never grow tired of each other, either. All our rough edges will be smoothed out.

Ask God to help you be more patient with the foibles of others in this life. God loves us even now, as imperfect as we are; we should love one another the same way.

❧

GIVE THANKS TO THE GOD OF HEAVEN. HIS LOVE
ENDURES FOREVER.
—PSALM 136:26

62.
. . . And we'll never cease to be awed by Him.

Have you ever been around someone with a dynamic, magnetic, bigger-than-life personality? It's thrilling and energizing just to be near such a person. Elvis Presley, for instance, had teenagers screaming in their seats. So did the Fab Four. It would be an understatement to say that there was commotion in the TV studio in 1964 when Ed Sullivan announced, "Ladies and gentlemen, the Beatles!"

In a somewhat similar manner, power and authority evoke strong feelings of awe, reverence, and respect. The title President of the United States is so highly regarded that every member of Congress rises to their feet when the one holding that office enters the room to deliver the State of the Union address. Can you imagine how thrilled you'd be to stand close enough to shake hands with the president as he makes his way to the podium?

However, these examples are nothing compared with the excitement of heaven, because there we'll be in the presence of Almighty God himself! He is the source of all energy and vitality and creativity, a God of infinite ability and power and intellect and beauty. Psalm 89:6–7 says, "Who is like the LORD among the heavenly beings? In the council of the holy ones God is greatly feared; he is more awesome than all who surround him." As incredible as we and the angels will be in heaven, God will always be more awesome by far.

As you meditate on the Bible, ask God to reveal to you more of His glory. The more you appreciate God's greatness, the closer you are to heaven.

❧

O LORD, MY GOD, HOW GREAT YOU ARE!
YOU ARE CLOTHED WITH MAJESTY AND GLORY.
—PSALM 104:1 TEV

63.
In heaven we'll fulfill our highest calling.

God's greatest command is to love Him (Matthew 22:37–38). We begin to fulfill this, our highest calling, in our earthly life through faith. But our greatest realization of it will be in eternity. Earth is the proving ground for our love for God; heaven is the place where we'll fully express to our Heavenly Father the depth of our love.

Many years ago Danish philosopher and theologian Søren Kierkegaard wrote a story about a king in love with a peasant girl. He loved her in spite of her rags and wanted her to love him apart from his riches. The gap between them was so great, he realized there was only one way they could ever be married. So he renounced his throne and became a villager himself in order to woo her. He knew there was no guarantee he would win her heart, but he loved her so much that he was willing to take this risk.

Kierkegaard didn't reveal the outcome of his tale, because it's a parable, the story of God's relationship with humankind.

The Lord hides His splendor from us for now, hoping we'll love Him for who He is and not merely for what He can offer us. If we agree to become His,

He'll bring us to His opulent royal palace in heaven, dress us in the finest of clothes, and place a crown upon our head. And there we'll enjoy a blessed union with Him forevermore.

First Peter 1:8 CEV says, "You have never seen Jesus, and you don't see him now. But still you love him and have faith in him." Your best opportunity to prove to God that you love Him is right here, right now, in this life on earth. It will be easy to love and trust Him in heaven, where you'll see Him face-to-face. Show the Lord that you believe in Him and love Him today—He wants to know it before you see Him in all His glory! It's this kind of faith that truly pleases God (Hebrews 11:6).

❧

LOVE THE LORD YOUR GOD WITH ALL YOUR HEART
AND WITH ALL YOUR SOUL AND WITH ALL YOUR MIND
AND WITH ALL YOUR STRENGTH.
—MARK 12:30

64.
Your soul's greatest longing will be satisfied.

At the deepest level, we're all crying out, "My soul thirsts for God, for the living God. When can I go and meet with God?" (Psalm 42:2). This longing has been described as a God-shaped hole in our heart. At times the hole seems rather small, as if our heart were a jigsaw puzzle missing just one of a thousand tiny pieces. But sometimes the void feels like a chasm the size of the Grand Canyon. And there are times when the emptiness is so vast, it seems our inner universe is dominated by a gaping black hole.

The size of our need for God never changes, only our awareness of how deep it truly is. Likewise, the magnitude of God never varies, only our perception of His greatness. He is always sufficient to meet our need. The apostle Paul wrote, "I pray that you, being rooted and established in love, may have power, together with all the saints, to grasp how wide and long and high and deep is the love of Christ, and to know this love that surpasses knowledge—that you may be filled to the measure of all the fullness of God" (Ephesians 3:17–19). In heaven we will exist in God's presence, surrounded by His love, and our thirst for Him will be completely satisfied.

Don't wait for eternity to meet with God. Because of Christ's work on the cross, and because the Holy Spirit lives within us, we always have access to our Father in heaven. You may not see Him face-to-face, but you can be close to Him in spirit and begin to find joy, peace, and wholeness.

❧

WE WILL ALL BE WITH THE LORD FOREVER.
—1 THESSALONIANS 4:17 CEV

65.
Heaven has a great exchange policy.

The Lord will take all your sorrow and pain and replace it with blessing and joy. He'll give you "beauty for ashes, joy instead of mourning, praise instead of despair" (Isaiah 61:3 NLT). God will lift your downcast face to His, and He'll replace your sadness with a smile. He'll take the tears from your eyes and put a sparkle in their place!

We can't trade in every suffering here on earth, but we take a giant step toward heaven when, like Job, we praise God through our hurts, trusting Him to one day redeem them all.

❧

YOU TURNED MY WAILING INTO DANCING; YOU
REMOVED MY SACKCLOTH AND CLOTHED ME WITH JOY.
—PSALM 30:11

66.
You'll always feel a sense of belonging.

One of God's greatest promises is, "You will be my people, and I will be your God" (Jeremiah 30:22). This is so important to God that He repeated the promise again and again. The Lord had this relationship in mind from the very beginning. He created the union of a man and a woman as an illustration of it, and He often referred to this illustration throughout Scripture. In a marriage, spouses belong to each other. Song of Songs 6:3 MSG says it clearly: "I am my lover's and my lover is mine." Two people bound by love and marriage identify deeply with one another and experience an abiding sense of intimacy. In heaven, you'll never wonder to whom you belong.

If there's a question in your mind as to whether you belong to God today, now is the best time to place your faith in Jesus and settle the issue for all time.

❧

THE HOME OF GOD IS NOW AMONG HIS PEOPLE! HE
WILL LIVE WITH THEM, AND THEY WILL BE HIS PEOPLE.
—REVELATION 21:3 NLT

67.
Everyone will treat you like family.

When you step into heaven, it will be wonderful to be lovingly greeted by family members already there. But the other inhabitants of paradise aren't going to regard you as a stranger! Heaven will not be a collection of isolated family reunions. Every person there is God's child, and we'll all embrace each other, greeting one another with holy kisses, rejoicing and celebrating that God's family is together forever.

Galatians 6:10 says, "Let us do good to all people, especially to those who belong to the family of believers." Move closer to heaven today by treating everyone in this world like family. Some may be Christians now; some may be Christians someday. The way you treat nonbelievers may help them decide to join the family of God.

❧

To all who received him, to those who believed in his name, he gave the right to become children of God.
—John 1:12

68.
Your life will be complete.

In the presence of God, surrounded by all His glory, all His angels, all His children, and all the endless, unimaginable wonders of heaven, can you picture yourself musing, *Something's missing; there must be more to life?* If you could think of something that God hasn't already provided—which is impossible—surely He would be happy to give it to you. Psalm 145:16 NKJV says, "You open Your hand and satisfy the desire of every living thing," and in heaven there will be no reason for God to withhold anything from us.

Life can seem unfulfilling at times, but Jesus said that if we abide in His love now, as we will for eternity in heaven, He will make our joy complete (John 15:9–11).

🌿

I CAME SO THEY CAN HAVE REAL AND ETERNAL LIFE,
MORE AND BETTER LIFE THAN THEY EVER DREAMED OF.
—JOHN 10:10 MSG

69.
You'll always feel like a winner.

You'll never feel like a loser in heaven. You'll feel like a champion, because God will make you a champion (1 John 5:1–5)!

Jesus said, "In this world you will have trouble. But take heart! I have overcome the world" (John 16:33). Christ has already fought the battle and won the prize. He's invited you to join His team in the victory parade and share in the eternal reward.

❧

THANKS BE TO GOD! HE GIVES US THE VICTORY
THROUGH OUR LORD JESUS CHRIST.
—1 CORINTHIANS 15:57

70.
You'll learn who you really are.

God knows something you don't. He knows your true identity, the real you. He's known it from the beginning, since before He made you—even before He created the world (Psalm 139; Jeremiah 1:5; Ephesians 1:4). It's strange to think that the Lord knows more about us than we know about ourselves, but it's true.

When you think about this, it makes sense. Who really knows you? Surely not your acquaintances, who met you only a short while ago. Close friends may have shared a good deal of your life, but not all. Brothers and sisters, even parents, have known you only since the moment of your birth. And by the time you became aware of yourself, in the womb, you'd already passed through many stages of development; even at that early point in your creation, you were already "marvelously made" (Psalm 139:14 MSG) by a loving, knowing God.

People live out their lives trying to find themselves, struggling deep inside with the question, "Who am I?" We learn some things about ourselves as we grow and mature, but until we leave this life and step into heaven, the essence of our identity is never fully revealed to us.

In human terms, history often has the final say in judging a person's identity. It's only years after the death of a famous man or woman that historians, who feel they've finally gathered all the facts and have the perspective that comes with the passage of time, can declare with any real sense of confidence who this person was, what his or her impact on the world may have been. Even then, the issue remains unresolved, as history continues to be rewritten.

But God, the righteous Judge, does more than evaluate our identity; He determined it. The answer to the question, "Who am I?" is already sealed in the annals of eternity. In fact, it's written in stone.

In heaven, the Bible promises, God will hand us this stone. It's white—perhaps it's a beautifully polished marble plaque—and has our true name engraved on it, the name that identifies us thoroughly, the name that defines our existence from the perfect, eternal perspective of our omniscient Lord.

The amazing thing is, when we see our new name, when we hear it spoken, we'll smile wide with instant recognition, as if we've known it all along! Our true name will feel right; it will fit. We'll spend eternity with a rich, secure sense of identity. The burning question deep in our heart will be replaced with the sure knowledge, "This is who I am."

Scott was twelve when his parents' divorce split his world in two. His mother sold their large home in the suburbs and moved the family to an old farmhouse out in the country. Occasionally his father would fly into the small rural airport in a corporate jet and whisk Scott and his siblings out of state for a visit.

There Scott stayed in his father's high-rise condo in the heart of a large metropolitan city. As a teenager, Scott wasn't sure to which world he belonged.

When he graduated from high school and started college, Scott's identity crisis became more acute. Suddenly the question, "What do I want to be when I grow up?" was no longer hypothetical but needed to be answered. Yet he didn't really know who he was, where he was coming from, what his parents' expectations were, or what resources were available to him to help pay for his education. He didn't know himself.

This lack of identity resulted in low self-esteem, and Scott fell into a pattern of changing his major area of study, attending college for a couple of years, dropping out of school to work for a while, and then reentering the university to begin the cycle all over again. He was a good student with a high grade-point average, but fear of failure kept causing him to quit.

Finally Scott gave up on school completely. He managed to find a job with what seemed to be a promising future, and for a few years he was somewhat content, except he regretted never finishing his degree, and he sensed he wasn't doing with his life what he was meant to do. His work didn't provide him the personal satisfaction and fulfillment he needed, and he kept wondering, *Who am I?*

That question prompted Scott to begin looking for God. As he learned more about the Lord, he began learning more about himself—not in terms of career choice and vocation but in terms of the common identity we all share as beings created by a loving Father. Eventually Scott committed his life to God, and soon afterward the Lord began revealing to him something of his unique, individual identity. Scott began to realize that his longtime love of drawing and illustration, and the arts in general, was an indication of the kind of person God had created him to be. He'd stopped drawing pictures after high school, when he got busy following one career path after another. But suddenly it became clear to him that God had designed him to be an artist. Scott wondered why he hadn't seen this in himself before, because it made so much sense to him now. It felt right; it fit.

These days Scott has his own business, working out of an office in his home. His biggest struggle currently is juggling the responsibilities that come with being a successful freelance illustrator, a loving husband, an involved father, a dedicated member of his church, and an active citizen in his community. He feels richly blessed that God has given him not one but several identities! At the same time, he's aware that the Lord's plan for his life continues to unfold day by day, as God reveals to him more and more of the person he was created to be. In a very real sense, Scott is still finding himself.

Sometimes Scott wonders about the secret name God has chosen for him, the one he will learn about in heaven, the name that represents the totality of who he is and how his life fits into God's grand design for history and humanity. Somehow Scott knows that his new name will be, at least in part, a family name, one that forever identifies him as God's child.

Many people in the Bible received new identities from God: Saul became Paul, Jacob became Israel,

Abram became Abraham, Simon became Peter. Before he fought a single battle, Gideon—the least man in his family, which was of the weakest clan in his tribe—was called, "mighty warrior" (Judges 6:12). As you walk with God in this life, ask Him to begin to show you who you really are.

❧

I WILL ALSO GIVE EACH OF THEM A WHITE STONE ON WHICH IS WRITTEN A NEW NAME THAT NO ONE KNOWS EXCEPT THE ONE WHO RECEIVES IT.
—REVELATION 2:17 TEV

71.
You'll discover your legacy.

Rick Warren, author of *The Purpose-Driven Life*, writes, "Many people spend their lives trying to create a lasting legacy on earth. They want to be remembered when they're gone. Yet, what ultimately matters most will not be what others say about your life but what God says. . . . Living to create an earthly legacy is a short-sighted goal. A wiser use of time is to build an eternal legacy."

In this lifetime, we'll never really know the lasting effect we have on others. But in heaven our eternal legacy will be revealed to us. It will be in print, right there in black and white, for our biographies have already been published in heaven. Psalm 139:16 TEV says, "The days allotted to me had all been recorded in your book, before any of them ever began." It's one of God's mysteries that without controlling our will, He knows our actions beforehand. But the Lord exists apart from time, and somehow He sees now what we'll be doing in the future, as if He watches us do it.

What will your eternal legacy be? There is one way to ensure that it will be one worth remembering: dedicate your life to God. If you do, He'll use you in powerful ways, and He'll make your reputation great.

You'll be forever known as a pillar of God's temple (Revelation 3:12).

✤

COMMIT YOUR WAY TO THE LORD; TRUST IN HIM
AND HE WILL DO THIS: HE WILL MAKE YOUR RIGHT-
EOUSNESS SHINE LIKE THE DAWN, THE JUSTICE OF
YOUR CAUSE LIKE THE NOONDAY SUN.
—PSALM 37:5–6

72.
You'll always have peace.

As you spend eternity with Jesus in heaven, you'll know true peace, because "he himself is our peace" (Ephesians 2:14). In fact, Jesus is the Prince of Peace (Isaiah 9:6)—there's no greater peace to be found!

The Hebrew word for peace, shalom, is traditionally used as a greeting or farewell among Jewish people, and it conveys more than just the notion of serenity and contentment. It also carries the concept of completeness or soundness. Biblical peace is more than just peace of mind or lack of stress; it's a wholeness of body, mind, and spirit.

In this world, people try all sorts of methods to find peace. But the Bible gives us several surefire ways to find it: trust God (Isaiah 26:3); rejoice in Him always (Philippians 4:4); pray instead of worrying (Philippians 4:6-7); and focus on what's good in this world—the positive, excellent, praiseworthy things that please God (Philippians 4:8-9). If we take these steps by faith, Jesus will begin to give us a peace that the world can't offer. It's a powerful kind of peace that will help us to weather the storms of life, to endure heavy winds and emerge intact.

"The Lord bless you and keep you; the Lord make His face shine upon you, and be gracious to you; the Lord lift up His countenance upon you, and give you peace."
—Numbers 6:24–26 NKJV

73.
We'll find our lost innocence.

Contrary to popular notion, we were not born innocent. Our innocence was lost for us, long ago, by Adam and Eve, our first ancestors.

The moment we place our faith in Jesus, His sacrifice makes us innocent in God's eyes, but we still carry the burden of sinfulness for the rest of our earthly lives. It's the Holy Spirit's job to work in our hearts until the day we stand before our holy God, truly innocent.

When Jesus said we must become childlike to enter the kingdom of heaven (Matthew 18:3), He was not talking about innocence—that is, the kind of innocence we might try to achieve on our own. He was talking about humility and trust. God can and will make us innocent if we only humble ourselves and trust Him.

How magnificent it will feel someday to be completely innocent and trusting! In this world, it seems too risky to trust. We learn to keep our guard up. But in heaven we'll be able to drop our defenses and live carefree for all eternity. We'll be free to be open and honest with people we've never met, with no fear of physical or emotional harm, for everyone in heaven will be innocent like us. We'll be free to love God and others without worrying about getting hurt. We'll be free to be ourselves, the way we were always meant to be.

Developing a childlike trust in God becomes easier as you get to know Him more and grow to realize that your faith in Him is well placed.

❧

"LET THE LITTLE CHILDREN COME TO ME, AND DO NOT
HINDER THEM, FOR THE KINGDOM OF GOD BELONGS
TO SUCH AS THESE."
—MARK 10:14

74.
You'll always feel rested.

As we travel through this world, some days we're full of vigor. We've had a good night's rest and feel unstoppable, ready for anything! Then there are those days when we feel drained, lethargic. We didn't get the rest we need and now we lack energy. Well, there won't be any days like those as we wander through heaven, exploring its wonders, because it's a place of eternal rest. All our days there will be "up" days!

Isaiah 40:31 TEV says, "Those who trust in the LORD for help will find their strength renewed. They will rise on wings like eagles; they will run and not get weary; they will walk and not grow weak." We spiritual pilgrims can find relief for our tired souls today, and new vitality, by going to Jesus, who promised to give us rest, show us the way, and lighten our load for the journey (Matthew 11:28–30).

❧

WE WHO BELIEVE, THEN, DO RECEIVE THAT REST
WHICH GOD PROMISED.
—HEBREWS 4:3 TEV

75.
You'll never have to lock your door.

Nobody locks their doors in paradise! The impressive city gates are always left wide open, allowing everyone to come and go whenever they please. There's no need for security lights, since it never gets dark. Besides, there are no crooks in heaven (only former thieves).

It's a secure place for adults, and it's also child-proofed, perfectly safe even for toddlers. Isaiah 11:8–9 says, "The infant will play near the hole of the cobra, and the young child put his hand into the viper's nest. They will neither harm nor destroy on all my holy mountain, for the earth will be full of the knowledge of the LORD." We could ask for a better world for ourselves, we could ask for a better world in which to bring up our kids, but we could never ask for a better God. He'll care for us and them, now and always. Take a step toward heaven today by giving all your worries to the Lord, whether they concern you or your children.

❧

ON NO DAY WILL ITS GATES EVER BE SHUT, FOR THERE WILL BE NO NIGHT THERE.
—REVELATION 21:25

76.
You'll finally, fully understand the gospel message.

An earnest, sincere Christian struggles alone up a lofty mountain. It's his area of greatest temptation and sin, and he's striving to conquer it, to plant a white flag of victory atop it. The climb is difficult, but he presses on. He imagines himself someday standing before his beloved Jesus, pointing at this flag, and all his little white flags on the lesser mountains below, and saying, "Lord, look what I've done for You!"

However, as he tries to scale this monstrous summit, he repeatedly stumbles and falls, until, lying there exhausted, he notices that his flag is no longer white. Instead it's tattered, torn, dirty. He finally realizes he can't win this battle, and at that moment Jesus appears beside him and helps him to his feet. The Lord takes the small ruined flag, tucks it into the folds of His robe, and with a nail-scarred hand indicates a glorious white banner at the peak of the mountain. Smiling, Jesus says, "Look what I've done for you." Then He shoulders the man's backpack, points out a better path, and begins helping him up the slope. On the day we enter heaven, each of us will finally grasp the truth of Isaiah 64:6 NLT, which says, "When we proudly display our righteous deeds, we find they are but filthy rags." Only then will we fully understand what good news the gospel really is!

Ask the Lord to help you begin letting go of your little white flags, giving them to Him, so you can stand with Him under His pure white banner of victory.

❧

YOU WERE SAVED BY FAITH IN GOD. . . . THIS IS GOD'S GIFT TO YOU, AND NOT ANYTHING YOU HAVE DONE ON YOUR OWN.
—EPHESIANS 2:8 CEV

77.
We'll stand in the epicenter of love.

Have you ever had a sense of the magnitude of God's love? Have you felt the depth of His desire, the fiery passion that burns in His heart, blazing forth as if to consume us?

First Samuel 6:20 says, "Who can stand in the presence of the LORD?" When Isaiah came before God, he cried out, "Woe is me, for I am undone!" (Isaiah 6:5 NKJV). Isaiah was responding as a sinful man in the presence of holiness. As Christians, we trust Jesus to take away our sins and make us worthy to stand before God. But our Heavenly Father radiates more than just holiness. Are we prepared to experience the pure, raw power of His love?

Just hearing about God's love, listening to a testimony of how He has graciously touched someone's life, can be extremely moving, overwhelming our emotions and melting our hearts. How can we hope to behold God himself and receive the full force of His love, without crumbling to pieces or being blown completely away?

The amazing thing is, with Jesus by our side, we will be able to withstand the intensity of our Father's love, and it will be like basking in the warmth of the sun.

First John 4:7 MSG says, "My beloved friends, let us continue to love each other since love comes from God." The more we abide in love, the more at home we will feel in God's presence.

🌱

God is love. When we take up permanent residence in a life of love, we live in God and God lives in us.
—1 John 4:16 MSG

78.
We'll hear the tender thunder of God's voice.

In the Bible, God's voice is described as "loud," "powerful," "majestic," "like a trumpet," "like the roar of rushing waters," "like thunder." Yet He also speaks in "a gentle whisper," "tenderly," even "with singing." It's difficult to imagine such a voice, but someday in heaven we'll experience it ourselves, and it will be the most wonderful sound we've ever heard.

Although we must wait to hear our Father's voice, we can listen to Him right now—through the Scriptures, especially Jesus' words; through other Christians, especially those gifted in preaching and teaching; and through the Holy Spirit, especially during prayer. God may be silent today, but He is not incommunicado! And His message is "sweeter than honey."

Time and again Jesus said, "He who has ears, let him hear." You take a step toward heaven the moment you begin to listen.

❧

THE MESSAGE IS VERY CLOSE AT HAND; IT IS ON YOUR
LIPS AND IN YOUR HEART SO THAT YOU CAN OBEY IT.
—DEUTERONOMY 30:14 NLT

79.
When we meet God, He won't be a stranger . . .

How do we get to know someone, understand their personality, evaluate their character, find out who they really are? We look in their eyes. We observe their facial expressions. We listen to their words and the tone of their voice. We watch what they do. We witness their interactions with others. We spend time with them and pay attention to how they treat us. We share our heart with them and give them the opportunity to share their heart with us.

Part of the reason God became a human being was so we could get to know Him. Jesus told His disciples, "Now that you have known me . . . you will know my Father also, and from now on you do know him and you have seen him. . . . Whoever has seen me has seen the Father" (John 14:7, 9 TEV). The mysterious, invisible God of the universe wanted us to see His face and hear His voice and know His heart, so that when we finally stand before Him one day in heaven, it will be like seeing an old friend.

We grow closer to God by getting to know Jesus Christ. God has provided several ways for us to do this. We can learn more about Jesus by reading and meditating on the Gospel accounts of His life. We can understand Jesus better by listening to those who are gifted in teaching and preaching God's Word. We can experience Jesus' presence through community with other believers within the body of Christ, His church. And we can enjoy deep, personal fellowship with Jesus and know Him intimately by allowing His Spirit to reside within us.

❧

THE SON IS THE RADIANCE OF GOD'S GLORY AND THE EXACT REPRESENTATION OF HIS BEING.
—HEBREWS 1:3

80.
. . . And Jesus will not have changed a bit.

A woman arrived at the place where her class reunion was being held. There were several banquet rooms in the building, and she wasn't sure which to enter. When she poked her head through the first doorway, she saw a roomful of elderly-looking people and immediately decided this couldn't be it. Then one of the old folks came over to her and welcomed her by name! Often when we encounter someone we haven't seen in years, it's startling to discover how much they've changed. Outward, physical differences are the first things we notice, and these can take some getting used to. Inner, deeper changes are more difficult to spot, but they're the ones that have greater impact, for better or for worse.

Although it's been over two thousand years since Jesus walked the earth, we needn't fear that He's different in any way. And no matter how long it takes before we're all gathered together in heaven, time will have no effect on Him. Like His Father, Christ does not change (James 1:17). Throughout eternity, He will always be our Good Shepherd, our Wonderful Counselor, our Great High Priest, Our loving Savior and Lord.

Jesus is as solid as a rock, and so is His Word. If you build your life on His promises, your home will rest securely on a firm foundation (Matthew 7:24–25).

❧

JESUS CHRIST *IS* THE SAME YESTERDAY, TODAY,
AND FOREVER.
—HEBREWS 13:8 NKJV

81.
All Christians will make it to heaven.

Not one person can reach heaven without Jesus. But that's precisely the reason we can be certain we'll all get there with Him! Romans 3:23–24 says, "All have sinned and fall short of the glory of God, and are justified freely by his grace through the redemption that came by Christ Jesus." From the most ardent believer to the least pious among us, Jesus saves everyone who calls on His name.

However, what we do with our life after we put our trust in Jesus matters greatly. It's possible to build on the foundation of Christ yet end up with a structure that has no lasting value. Christians do this when they focus all their energy on building up things like wealth, notoriety, or material possessions.

God's Word says the quality of our life's work will be tested one day with fire. If we've built wisely, we'll be rewarded. If we've built foolishly, we'll still make it to heaven, but only "like someone escaping from flames" (1 Corinthians 3:15 CEV). We'll lose the temporary things we've worked so hard to accumulate.

All Christians will make it to heaven, but there may be quite a few there with singed eyebrows, having nothing to show for their lives but the smell of smoke about them! You can avoid being one of them by living your life in light of eternity, striving for those things that retain their value forever.

❧

WHOSOEVER SHALL CALL ON THE NAME OF THE LORD
SHALL BE DELIVERED.
—JOEL 2:32 KJV

82.

Jesus won't recognize everyone who knocks at heaven's door . . .

What will be the Lord's tone of voice as He turns away a stranger at the gates of heaven? What will be the expression on His face? Will His tone be stern, His expression angry? Or might there not be a sigh in His voice, a tear in His eye?

Jesus once lamented, "O Jerusalem, Jerusalem, . . . how often I have longed to gather your children together, as a hen gathers her chicks under her wings, but you were not willing" (Matthew 23:37). The Lord wants so much to know you! Turn a willing heart toward Him now, while there's still time to get acquainted.

🍃

"Not everyone who says to me, 'Lord, Lord,' will enter the kingdom of heaven, but only he who does the will of my Father who is in heaven. Many will say to me on that day, 'Lord, Lord, did we not prophesy in your name, and in your name drive out demons and perform many miracles?' Then I will tell them plainly, 'I never knew you.'"

—Matthew 7:21–23

83.
. . . But He'll recognize His own.

Will Jesus know His brother standing at His door, regardless of how much time has passed? Will He recognize His sister, though years of estrangement have taken their toll? At once! He'll throw open the door and happily welcome them in, because they are family, because they belong to Him.

If you're a lost sheep, a Christian who's strayed from the faith, you need never be afraid to come back to Jesus. It doesn't matter how far you've wandered; He will greet you with a warm embrace.

❧

"I AM THE GOOD SHEPHERD. AS THE FATHER KNOWS ME AND I KNOW THE FATHER, IN THE SAME WAY I KNOW MY SHEEP AND THEY KNOW ME."
—JOHN 10:14 TEV

84.
Getting into heaven means doing the impossible.

Jesus said, "Dear children, it is very hard to get into the Kingdom of God" (Mark 10:24 NLT). He pointed out that it's particularly difficult for well-to-do people, saying it would be easier for a camel to pass through the eye of a needle than for a person of means to step through the gates of heaven.

The disciples knew that Jesus wasn't merely talking about the super-rich. Most of us are far wealthier than we realize! They asked Jesus in astonishment, "Then who in the world can be saved?" (Mark 10:26 NLT).

Now, the "eye of a needle" that Jesus mentioned could actually have been a small gate for people, next to the much larger city gate. A camel might get through it by kneeling and struggling, but the poor animal would certainly need assistance. On the other hand, Jesus may indeed have been talking about a sewing needle, in which case getting a camel through would require divine intervention! Whichever allusion He intended, the meaning to us is clear: we can't get into heaven on our own.

Whether we're rich or not, the Bible says very plainly that anyone who doesn't meet God's standard of perfect holiness cannot enter paradise. It also states unequivocally that everyone falls short of meeting this requirement.

The bottom line is, for us the prospect of getting into heaven is an impossibility. Yet with Jesus' help it's a sure thing!

Jesus told a rich young ruler that he could get into heaven by selling what he owned, giving the money to the poor, and following Him. This sounds like harsh advice, but the man was struggling like a camel, and Jesus was trying to help. The Lord knew he loved his money and his things more than God, and his material things had to go. Jesus will help you into heaven, too, if you let Him show you to what extent you need to lighten your load.

❧

"ALL THINGS ARE POSSIBLE WITH GOD."
—MARK 10:27

85.
It takes faith to get to heaven, but not mindless faith.

All of us must take a step of faith to trust that Jesus is the only way to heaven. God hasn't given us absolute proof that the Bible is true. On the other hand, He has given us enough evidence so that taking that step is a perfectly reasonable, rational thing to do.

You don't have to abandon your intellect to have faith. Study the Bible carefully; God's truths will stand up under the most intense scrutiny. Consider the Lord's promises. Weigh the costs. Talk to others who have already taken the step. Talk it over with God himself—He has a reputation for being quite wise.

❦

"COME NOW, LET US REASON TOGETHER," SAYS THE
LORD. "THOUGH YOUR SINS ARE LIKE SCARLET, THEY
SHALL BE AS WHITE AS SNOW."
—ISAIAH 1:18

86.
Heaven is a white-tie affair.

Formal attire is required at God's great banquet (Matthew 22:11–12). Thankfully, it's also graciously provided. In heaven we'll receive beautiful white robes to wear. God will adorn us in "fine linen, bright and clean" (Revelation 19:8), so we'll be perfectly resplendent for the grand occasion. Despite the dress code, however, the atmosphere at the celebration will be anything but stuffy—in fact, it'll be downright jubilant!

This fine clothing God wants us to wear represents the righteous acts of believers (Revelation 19:8). We move closer to heaven when we realize that our good deeds qualify for this purpose only when they flow from God's righteousness within us—that is, the righteousness God gives us through faith in Jesus (Philippians 3:9).

🌱

THEY WERE CLOTHED IN WHITE AND HELD PALM BRANCHES IN THEIR HANDS. AND THEY WERE SHOUTING WITH A MIGHTY SHOUT, "SALVATION COMES FROM OUR GOD ON THE THRONE AND FROM THE LAMB!"
—REVELATION 7:9-10 NLT

87.
Heaven is a happening place!

Don't let the devil or anyone else fool you into thinking that paradise is a dull place filled with bored, listless people sitting on clouds and playing harps, while the real party is happening elsewhere. The Bible portrays heaven as a place of endless celebration, joy, pleasure, and delight.

C. S. Lewis wrote, "All the scriptural imagery (harps, crowns, gold, etc.) is, of course, a merely symbolical attempt to express the inexpressible. Musical instruments are mentioned because for many people (not all) music is the thing known in the present life which most strongly suggests ecstasy and infinity. Crowns are mentioned to suggest the fact that those who are united with God in eternity share His splendour and power and joy. Gold is mentioned to suggest the timelessness of Heaven (gold does not rust) and the preciousness of it."

God's Word also paints a true picture of the conditions down at Satan's little shindig. It's not quite the glamorous affair that Satan would like you to think it is.

And not only does it fail to live up to this propaganda, but the devil didn't even bother to send you an invitation. He's just assuming that you'll come. God, on the other hand, loves you so much that He took great pains to issue you a personal invite. He's also offered to provide everything you'll need to attend His royal banquet—particularly the right clothes to wear, because after all, we're going to be dancing and rejoicing in the presence of a King.

All God is waiting for is your response, so He can add your name to His list of guests, each of whom He will be expecting with delightful anticipation.

If you are the fun-loving, sociable type who loves to be where the action is, get your R.S.V.P. to God right away, accepting Jesus' invitation to eternal life. Otherwise you'll wind up dropping in at the devil's open house by default.

🍃

YOU WILL FILL ME WITH JOY IN YOUR PRESENCE, WITH
ETERNAL PLEASURES AT YOUR RIGHT HAND.
—PSALM 16:11

88.

There are some distinguished names on heaven's guest list— and it can include yours.

Matthew 8:11 MSG says those who are on the Lord's list will soon be "sitting down at God's kingdom banquet alongside Abraham, Isaac, and Jacob." These patriarchs, and other believers who have long ago left this earth, are with God in heaven at this very moment, alive and well, waiting for us to join them!

How do we know for sure these saints of old are living today in paradise? Jesus pointed out that His Father often identified himself as the God of Abraham, the God of Isaac, and the God of Jacob, and added, "He is not the God of the dead, but of the living, for to him all are alive" (Luke 20:37–38). We get a glimpse of this amazing truth at the Transfiguration, when long after their time Moses and Elijah are seen alive, talking with Jesus on the mountain (Matthew 17:1–3).

All men and women of faith who have gone before us are in heaven now, waiting for the rest of God's saints to make their grand entries. The good news for us is the Bible promises that anyone who trusts God's Word will also experience everlasting life, and take part in His eternal celebration.

Every person honored and privileged to be granted a seat at God's banquet table is certain to be in very good company. Is your name on the list?

❧

"BLESSED ARE THOSE INVITED TO THE WEDDING
SUPPER OF THE LAMB."
—REVELATION 19:9 MSG

89.

Every entry in the Book of Life looks like this: John Doe (1961–   ).

The terms *lifetime* and *forever* have become nearly synonymous. We frequently use them side by side, as if they meant the same thing. A lifetime membership means forever having access to the health club. A lifetime service plan provides freedom forever from worrying about repair bills. Lifetime guarantees, lifetime contracts, lifetime employment—we think about these as lasting forever.

A lifetime is a long time, but in our hearts we know it's not forever. And when we consider the things that matter to us most, we feel it's not nearly enough. How can two people in love be content with merely a lifetime together? How can parents ever be satisfied with only a lifetime to cherish and enjoy their children? All of us have eternity in our hearts. Every person, no matter how forlorn and dejected, has a deep desire to live and experience all life has to offer, and to never stop living.

Increasingly, people are leading accelerated lives, as though trying to cram two or more lifetimes into the limited number of days allotted them on earth. But that's not the abundant life Jesus promised His followers. A truly full life can mean nothing less than a life that never ends. We sense this intuitively, because God designed us with a longing for eternity. In paradise this yearning will finally be satisfied, for there God has removed all distinction between lifetime and forever.

Don't settle for merely seventy or eighty years of living and loving; reach out and take the free gift of full, abundant, everlasting life that Jesus is offering. Make sure your name is written in the Book of Life (Revelation 21:27), so you'll have an eternity in heaven to experience all the love God has for you.

❧

HE HAS PUT ETERNITY IN THEIR HEARTS.
—ECCLESIASTES 3:11 NKJV

90.
Paradise has nice perks.

How would you react if your employer announced that the company's new benefits package included one thousand days of vacation time? Better yet, imagine that you worked for one of the major airlines, and another perquisite allowed you to travel for free. You could spend nearly three years anywhere in the world!

As glorious as this sounds, if you are wise, you wouldn't hesitate an instant to trade this opportunity for just one day in heaven. A single day in paradise is more thrilling than a three-year expedition through the Himalayas.

The incredible thing is, God's benefit package includes not only one such day in heaven but an eternity of them! And living with the Lord in paradise forever is just one of the rewards He offers for signing on with Him. Best of all, God is always seeking new workers for His kingdom. He never rejects anyone's application!

🌿

BETTER IS ONE DAY IN YOUR COURTS THAN A THOU-
SAND ELSEWHERE.
—PSALM 84:10

91.
Shining shoes in heaven beats any career in hell.

What can you say about someone who accepts the free gift of salvation from Jesus, sticks it in his back pocket as if it were a ticket to heaven, then goes on about life with hardly another thought about God? It may be that Christ will turn him away as a stranger at the pearly gates (Matthew 7:21–23). But the Bible does say that everyone who calls on Jesus' name will be saved (Acts 2:21), so perhaps the Lord will open the gates after all.

Will He do so begrudgingly? No! Christ will welcome this person into paradise with tears of joy and a warm embrace. And this person will have so much more to be thankful for because he will know more than ever that the gifts of God come from His grace.

Jesus understood this principle when He forgave the woman who washed His feet with her tears. He noted that her love was greater because she was forgiven much (Luke 7:40-47).

If you have days when you feel like you can't qualify for even doorkeeping in Heaven, don't let that discourage you. Jesus has not only covered your sin with His sacrifice, but He promises to help you overcome sin's power in your life. Your ticket is more than a piece of paper that gets you into Heaven if you keep your nose clean. It empowers you to live the kind of life you'll live in heaven—right now!

Whatever you've done with the ticket Jesus gave you, take a close look at it now and consider what it means.

I WOULD RATHER BE A DOORKEEPER IN THE HOUSE OF MY GOD THAN DWELL IN THE TENTS OF WICKEDNESS.
—PSALM 84:10 NKJV

92.
Heaven is more valuable than all the riches of earth . . .

Jesus compared God's kingdom to a treasure worth everything you have. Heaven is worth selling your house, your car, your home entertainment system, your jewelry, your clothes, your investment portfolio—all your possessions! It's even worth giving up your life.

Jim Elliot, a missionary who was martyred trying to bring the gospel message to the Auca Indians of Ecuador, wrote in his journal, "He is no fool who gives what he cannot keep to gain what he cannot lose."

Heaven is so precious because it endures forever. After all, when you really stop to think about it, what good is anything that doesn't last? C. S. Lewis noted, "All that is not eternal is eternally useless."

Another reason why heaven is so valuable is that it cost God so much. In reality, we couldn't buy our way into paradise with all the money in the world. We couldn't earn our way into heaven even if we laid down our lives, without faith in Jesus. The price of heaven is nothing less than the blood of Christ (1 Peter 1:18–19). In light of that, it makes the utmost sense for us to do whatever it takes to appropriate for ourselves the benefit of Jesus' sacrifice.

We place high priority on the things we value most, things that carry the greatest price. Although eternal life is given to us free of charge, take time to consider its value and what it cost Jesus to purchase it for us. Reflecting on the Gospel accounts of the Crucifixion, or seeing a movie like *The Passion of the Christ*, can deepen our appreciation for the value of heaven, our love for the Savior who suffered so much to redeem us, and our willingness to make whatever sacrifices we need to make to respond to Him fully and receive the gift of life everlasting.

❧

"THE KINGDOM OF HEAVEN IS LIKE A TREASURE
HIDDEN IN THE FIELD, WHICH A MAN FOUND AND HID
AGAIN; AND FROM JOY OVER IT HE GOES AND SELLS ALL
THAT HE HAS AND BUYS THAT FIELD."
—MATTHEW 13:44 NASB

93.
. . . And this treasure lasts forever.

If you've ever lost something to theft, insects, or corrosion, you can take comfort in knowing that nothing will be lost in heaven. A young man went to his mother's funeral. His job consisted of extensive travel, and he'd seldom made time to see her. It had been many years since he'd been home.

After the service, he went to her house to settle her affairs and prepare for the estate sale. As he entered the large, expansive home, damp and musty odors assaulted his nostrils. Dust was everywhere. It looked as though the housekeeper had left a decade ago. The velvet curtains were ragged, and the linen was being eaten by moths.

In the garage, his father's 1966 Ford pickup sat next to his mother's beautiful black Cadillac. Neither had been touched in years. No one had driven his father's truck since his death twelve years earlier. Rust had corroded the fenders, and the tires on the old pickup were flat.

Although his parents had set aside a rather large inheritance for him, and the estate was worth several million dollars, the young man sensed he'd missed something significant that his parents had tried to communicate before they died.

Walking slowly upstairs, he remembered his mother talking a lot about heaven during his last phone conversations with her. He assumed that was exactly where she was now.

When he reached his mother's bedroom, his eyes fell upon the open Bible next to her bed. He read the large-print, red-letter words she'd highlighted: "But store up for yourselves treasures in heaven, where neither moth nor rust destroys, and where thieves do not break in or steal."

Suddenly he understood what his mother had meant when she said, "All the money and possessions that will one day be yours hold no candle to where I'm going. Heaven is my home."

The young man opened his heart and asked the Lord to come in and live. He, too, wanted to experience life in heaven—a life without loss. He would see his parents again, with the Lord, and tell them all that he finally understood the true treasure of the eternal kingdom.

We take a step toward heaven when we understand that our future there is so much better than anything we experience here on earth.

❧

"STORE UP FOR YOURSELVES TREASURES IN HEAVEN, WHERE NEITHER MOTH NOR RUST DESTROYS, AND WHERE THIEVES DO NOT BREAK IN OR STEAL."
—MATTHEW 6:20 NASB

94.
Heaven is for sinners.

If you feel unworthy of God's kingdom, take heart! Heaven may be full of saints, but it's meant for sinners. The truth is, you don't get to be a saint until you recognize that you are a sinner. So if, when you're honest with yourself, you admit you're anything but righteous and holy, you're much closer to heaven than you realize.

In Luke 18:9–14, Jesus tells a parable about two types of people: those who feel justified by their own good deeds, and those who cry out to God for forgiveness. Heaven exists for the latter. Christ said it's humble sinners, not proud "saints," who are justified in God's eyes.

Admitting to God that you're a sinner may feel like a huge step down, but in truth it's a giant step up, for, as Jesus said, "he who humbles himself will be exalted" (Luke 18:14).

❧

"BLESSED ARE THE POOR IN SPIRIT,
FOR THEIRS IS THE KINGDOM OF HEAVEN."
—MATTHEW 5:3

95.
Christ makes you worthy of heaven.

Did you know that diamonds can be fingerprint-ed? They can, because each one has a distinct pattern of inclusions, or flaws, within it. When a laser beam passes through a diamond, the image it projects resembles a tiny universe of stars and constellations, representing the jewel's unique set of imperfections. This image can be recorded and kept on file in case it's ever needed to identify the gemstone.

Clarity, or purity, is one important measure of a diamond's value. The fewer inclusions a stone has, the greater its clarity, and the greater its worth. There are diamonds that have few flaws and are very valuable, but in this world you will never find a diamond that is perfectly pure.

If diamonds were people, the most precious stone on earth would be unacceptable to God. The Bible says only the pure in heart will see Him (Matthew 5:8). Anyone whose heart is the least bit impure is unworthy to be in God's presence.

The miracle of heaven is, Jesus makes "diamonds in the rough" like us into saints who are absolutely flawless, and priceless in God's sight!

First John 1:9 NKJV says, "If we confess our sins,

He is faithful and just to forgive us *our* sins and to cleanse us from all unrighteousness." Because of Christ's sacrifice on the Cross, one day you will stand unblemished before God in heaven, and as the splendor of His majesty shines upon you, the only image you'll reflect will be that of pure, radiant glory.

When we accept what Jesus has done for us, He makes us worthy of paradise.

❧

THE BLOOD OF JESUS, HIS SON, PURIFIES US FROM
EVERY SIN.
—1 JOHN 1:7 TEV

96.
God has a special seat reserved for you.

There's something special about arriving at a formal banquet and seeing a card on the table with your name printed on it. You realize that your host has been thinking of you, anticipating your presence, preparing for the time when you will sit down and enjoy a meal together on this grand occasion. As you take your seat, you feel honored, valued, knowing that somebody important considers you important too.

God himself, no one else—not even Jesus—has determined the seating arrangements at His great heavenly feast, and He's chosen a special place at the table just for you. Will you return the honor by reserving a place in your heart for Him?

❦

"TO SIT AT MY RIGHT OR LEFT IS NOT FOR ME TO GRANT. THESE PLACES BELONG TO THOSE FOR WHOM THEY HAVE BEEN PREPARED BY MY FATHER."
—MATTHEW 20:23

97.
Heaven works on the goldfish principle.

Remember when you asked your parents for a puppy, and they said, "First, let's see how you take care of a goldfish"? God's kingdom works the same way. Luke 16:10 says, "Whoever can be trusted with very little can also be trusted with much." The only difference is, things that are very little to God seem awfully big to us. When we ask, "Lord, give me true riches," He says, "First, let's see how you handle gold."

If you don't know God and aren't sure whether He's trustworthy, try trusting Him in the small things. He invites us to test Him, if our motives are right, and He will prove himself faithful.

❦

"WELL DONE, GOOD AND FAITHFUL SERVANT; YOU WERE FAITHFUL OVER A FEW THINGS, I WILL MAKE YOU RULER OVER MANY THINGS."
—MATTHEW 25:21 NKJV

98.
You can always get there from here.

They say the longest journey begins with a single step. For some people, the journey to heaven involves a lifetime of following Jesus. They start out with Christ when they're very young and never stop walking in His footsteps. Others take up the journey later in life, after traveling down other paths and discovering they lead nowhere. And there are those who become hopelessly lost in their wanderings, until it's nearly too late to change direction. For someone like the thief dying on the cross, who said, "Jesus, remember me when you come into your Kingdom" (Luke 23:42 NLT), a single step completes the entire journey.

It's better not to wait until the last minute to make a move toward heaven. But it's never too late in this life to take the one step that will get you there.

❧

JESUS ANSWERED HIM, "I TELL YOU THE TRUTH, TODAY
YOU WILL BE WITH ME IN PARADISE."
—LUKE 23:43

99.
It's all guaranteed!

The hope of heaven isn't wishful thinking. It's reliance on a solemn covenant. It's trust in a contract that has been signed and guaranteed. It's faith in a God who has proved that He always keeps His promises.

The Bible speaks of a hope that is certain (Hebrews 11:1). Jesus signed the contract through His sacrifice. When we sign our names through faith, God guarantees the promise through His Spirit.

❧

WHEN YOU BELIEVED IN CHRIST, HE IDENTIFIED YOU AS HIS OWN BY GIVING YOU THE HOLY SPIRIT, WHOM HE PROMISED LONG AGO. THE SPIRIT IS GOD'S GUARANTEE THAT HE WILL GIVE US EVERYTHING HE PROMISED.
—EPHESIANS 1:13–14 NLT

100.
We don't have long to wait.

At times this spiritual journey we're on, this quest for eternity, seems to last forever. It's as if we're walking along railroad tracks, watching the horizon, yearning to get to the place where the rails meet, but beginning to suspect they never will. Yet every railway line has an end, and each railroad tie we tread upon takes us one step closer to our destination.

Reaching eternity won't take an eternity! Psalm 39:5 NLT says, "Human existence is but a breath." Psalm 90:10 echoes this sentiment: "The length of our days is seventy years—or eighty, if we have the strength . . . they quickly pass, and we fly away." The older we get, the more we recognize this truth. Our time on earth is very short.

Also, Jesus repeatedly promised that He was coming soon. Who knows? As we continue our journey, gazing at the horizon, we may suddenly see a bright light appear. The Lord could meet us on the tracks tomorrow, gather us up, and carry us off to eternity like a high-speed bullet train!

The next step you take may be through the gates of heaven. How should you live in light of that truth? Romans 13:12 says, "The night is nearly over; the day is almost here. So let us put aside the deeds of darkness and put on the armor of light." If you haven't yet placed your faith in Jesus, there's no better time than now. If you're already a believer, Christ has made you a member of His family; you've been rescued from sin, set free to live out your life faithfully as a child of God.

♣

OUR SALVATION IS NEARER NOW THAN WHEN WE FIRST BELIEVED.
—ROMANS 13:11

101.
Heaven's gate is the door of your heart.

Heaven is truly an amazing place. And it's amazingly easy to get there. Christ said it's as simple as turning a lock on a door. When you open the door of your heart to Jesus, take a look over His shoulder: there lies paradise! In effect, you've cast wide the gates of heaven.

Someday soon Jesus will take you through that doorway to enjoy an eternity with Him in His home. In the meantime He will spend a lifetime with you in yours.

❧

LISTEN! I AM STANDING AND KNOCKING AT YOUR DOOR. IF YOU HEAR MY VOICE AND OPEN THE DOOR, I WILL COME IN AND WE WILL EAT TOGETHER.
—REVELATION 3:20 CEV

Bible Acknowledgments

Additional copies of this book are available
wherever good books are sold.

The following title is also available in this series:

101 Amazing Things God Says About You:
Discover Your God-given Purpose and Identity

❧

If you have enjoyed this book,
or if it has had an impact on your life,
we would like to hear from you.

Please contact us at

HONOR BOOKS
Cook Communications Ministries
4050 Lee Vance View
Colorado Springs, CO 80918

Or through our Web site

www.cookministries.com